To Eleanore
In His Great Love,
Norma Jean
& Wally (Ol' Glory Face)

IMPOSSIBLE MIRACLES

by Charles ♥♥ Frances Hunter

published by
Hunter Ministries Publishing Company
1600 Townhurst
Houston, Texas 77043

Canadian Office
Hunter Ministries Publishing Company of Canada
P.O. Box 30222, Station B
Calgary, Alberta, Canada T2M 4P1

1st Printing - Oct. 1976 25,000
2nd Printing - Aug. 1977 25,000

Scripture quotations are taken from:

The Authorized King James Version (KJV)
The Living Bible, Paraphrased. ©1971 by Tyndale House Publishers, Wheaton, Illinois. All references not specified are from The Living Bible.

ISBN 0-917726-05-7

It is impossible to understand God,
But we can understand him a little
When we see or hear of his
                    IMPOSSIBLE

                    MIRACLES!

OTHER HUNTER BOOKS:

TABLE OF CONTENTS

I CAN'T BELIEVE IT'S TRUE!

> And a vast crowd brought him their lame, blind, maimed, and those who couldn't speak, and many others, and laid them before Jesus, and he healed them all. What a spectacle it was! Those who hadn't been able to say a word before were talking excitedly, and those with missing arms and legs had new ones; the crippled were walking and jumping around, and those who had been blind were gazing about them! The crowds just marveled, and praised the God of Israel. (Matt. 15:30-31)

That really couldn't have happened, could it?

If it appeared in any book other than the Bible, maybe we couldn't believe it, but because it does appear in the Bible, we can believe it.

It happened because Jesus did it! Of course, that's the only way it could have happened.

But Jesus died.

Then his miracles must have stopped.

They would have, BUT . . . .

> Early on Sunday morning, as the new day was dawning, Mary Magdalene and the other Mary went out to the tomb. Suddenly there was a great earthquake; for an angel of the Lord came down from heaven and rolled aside the stone and sat on it. His face shone like lightning and his clothing was a brilliant white. The guards shook with fear when they saw him, and fell into a dead faint.

> Then the angel spoke to the women. "Don't be
> frightened!" he said, "I know you are looking for
> Jesus, who was crucified,
>
> BUT HE ISN'T HERE! FOR HE HAS COME
> BACK TO LIFE AGAIN, JUST AS HE SAID HE
> WOULD...." (Matt. 28:1-6)

Just as he said he would!

If that isn't impossible, we don't know what impossible means!

> JESUS CHRIST IS THE SAME YESTERDAY,
> TODAY, AND FOREVER. (Heb. 13:8)

Jesus lived before time was,

   Jesus lives today, and

      Jesus will live forever.

If he lives forever and today, he must still be doing the same kinds of miracles he did 2,000 years ago while he was living in a human body on earth. Jesus chose to live in a human body on earth, and uniquely, he has chosen to live today in a body — on earth. That sounds impossible, too, but it's in the Bible, so it must be true, just like those impossible miracles the Bible talked about in Matthew, and the impossibility of Jesus coming alive after he had been dead three days.

> I am crucified with Christ: nevertheless I live; yet
> not I, but Christ liveth in me: and the life which I
> now live in the flesh I live by the faith of the Son
> of God, who loved me, and gave himself for me.
> (Gal. 2:20 KJV)
>
> .... And this is the secret: that Christ in your
> hearts is your only hope of glory. (Col. 1:27b)

If we can have the faith of a little child, we can believe these impossible words of the Bible — words that say we who are living in a human body on earth are actually the body of Jesus! So, if we are the body of Jesus and he is the same today as when he did miracles, impossible miracles, then we in the human body should be able to do impossible miracles today, just as he did in his other earthly body.

What was it that gave him this awesome power to do all these wonderful, impossible miracles? It was God's mighty power, the power of the Holy Spirit, the power promised by Jesus to be given to his disciples — to us, his body. Jesus had the Spirit of the Living God in him to empower him to do these great and mighty acts of God. It was not until after Jesus was baptized in water and the Holy Spirit came down on him that he did anything unusual. His miracles started after the heavens were opened to him and he saw the Spirit of God coming down in the form of a dove.

> Don't you believe that I am in the Father and the Father is in me? The words I say are not my own but are from my Father who lives in me. And he does his work through me. Just believe it — that I am in the Father and the Father is in me. Or else believe it because of the mighty miracles you have seen me do. In solemn truth I tell you, anyone believing in me shall do the same miracles I have done, and even greater ones, because I am going to be with the Father. You can ask him for anything, using my name, and I will do it, for this will bring praise to the Father because of what I, the Son, will do for you. Yes, ask anything, using my name, and I will do it! (John 14:10-14)

If the Bible says it's true, then it IS true.

If your faith is strong enough to believe what we have said above, and strong enough to believe the Bible, then you have enough faith to believe some of the impossible miracles we want to share with you in this book. If your faith is not that strong, we want these true stories to build your faith for your own healing, healings through you, miracles in your own life, and miracles through you for others. But most of all, we want your faith to be absolute and firm in Jesus, the divine, living Son of God, who lives in and through us human beings on earth today by the mighty power of the Holy Spirit of God.

Come, walk along the Sea of Galilee, walk down the hillside, go with us to Capernaum as we climb into a boat, go off preaching in the cities like Jerusalem, or come walking on the water with us as we join Jesus on his journey through the world of miracles — impossible miracles. Come with us to Minneapolis, to Easton, to Green Bay, to Hackensack, to Gary . . . . . .

Come with us as Jesus lives in us and see him do his IMPOSSIBLE MIRACLES in the twentieth century. Let's go for a walk on spiritual water . . . . . . with Jesus!

NORMA JEAN VAN DELL

Norma Jean was fully qualified to have a visit from Jesus. She needed a visit from Jesus!

> Little children were brought for Jesus to lay his hands on them and pray. But the disciples scolded those who brought them. "Don't bother him," they said. But Jesus said, "Let the little children come to me, and don't prevent them. For of such is the Kingdom of Heaven." And he put his hands on their heads and blessed them before he left. (Matt. 19:13-15)

Jesus tells all of us to come to him with the faith of a little child, simply believing.

He wants us to trust him.

He wants us to have confidence in him.

He wants us to believe that he is just as real now as he was back then.

He wants to touch us with his hands and bless our lives.

Norma Jean was a little like Matthew. Matthew was a tax collector and Norma Jean prepared tax returns for her living. Matthew was a typical human being who didn't know Jesus and was disliked by most people because he was trying to please his human self by taking advantage of those over whom he had an advantage. Norma Jean wasn't trying to cheat in her job, but she was just as normal a human being as Matthew, and so she was just as qualified in her need for Jesus as was Matthew.

Jesus went to Matthew's house for dinner and there were many notorious swindlers there as guests. The Pharisees were indignant and wanted to know why Jesus associated with men like that.

Jesus said that people who are well don't need a doctor! It's sick people who do! Norma Jean then was qualified in more ways than one to need Jesus. First of all, she didn't really know Jesus enough to give all her life to him; secondly, she was sick.

So being qualified, she was ready for a visit from Jesus. But where was he? How could she find him among all the people in Minneapolis? She had found his old address before he moved from Jerusalem. She found his tracks in the Bible. But that was a long time ago and she needed to know where to find him now, in the twentieth century and in Minneapolis, not Jerusalem or out by a lake somewhere. And besides that, did she really believe he was available to meet her needs? With all the people he was with, how could she get his attention when she was just a common, ordinary, unknown person. She didn't really feel she was important enough for the Master to come to her house or even to her city. And even if he was there, would he stop to bless her when the crowds of sick people were pressing him, trying to just touch the hem of his garment! Besides all that, her afflictions were beyond the help of anyone. The doctors told her that. She was too far gone for any help from anyone in this world and hope was gone.

God said, "Seek me and you will find me."

Let's see how Norma Jean found this Jesus of Nazareth, whom people said could do impossible miracles — like she needed.

THIS IS MY STORY

by Norma Jean Van Dell

You really need a computer to list all the operations I have had since my first one before 1955.

This was an appendectomy. It left a scar, but really left me with no unusual problems. Lots of people have this operation and most people are hardly aware that a part of the body is missing. So it was with me, and I really didn't miss not having an appendix.

But I'll never forget my second one! In January, 1955, a truck ran into the back of our car causing an injury to my back. A disc in my spine slipped out into the spinal canal and ruptured, or herniated. It was swollen several times its normal size and was pressing on the nerve in my left leg, making walking very painful. The pain from the slipped disc went down through my hip, through the back of my leg and even into my toes. The doctors said if it was not taken care of I might not be able to walk at all.

Surgery, a laminectomy and a spinal fusion, was performed in May of that year. They removed the disc, took bone out of the back of my right hip and inserted it into the space where the disc was removed, so that it would grow to fill in the space.

The discs between vertebrae allow your back to bend, but when it has been fused, it doesn't bend at that point.

The surgery lasted four and a half hours. Before surgery, the doctors made a series of studies — discogram,

myelogram and spinogram, probing my spine. The spinogram test, as I understand it, is when they pumped the
fluid out of my spine and filled it with some purple dye.
This was done without an anesthetic, so I just "suffered it
out." The most painful was the discogram where they
insert a needle into each disc. For about forty-five minutes they tested each disc in three spaces, frequently
taking X-rays. When the needle touched the disc which
was ruptured it felt like my leg was electrocuted. It was
sheer torture, the worst pain I have ever endured. Even
after the operation, the pain was so terrible that I don't
think I could have lived through it except for the hypos. I
couldn't lie on my back or stomach. When they turned
me from one side to the other, it took two people about
twenty minutes. Because the pain was so excruciating, I
couldn't keep from screaming. I actually bent the metal
bridge in my mouth trying to bite hard enough not to
scream. This was the most horrible torture I could
imagine a human enduring.

This started a series of events and operations which
took me to a point of desperation and total despondency.
I had a total of ten operations in all. One year I had two!

I had surgery in 1955.
I had surgery in 1960.
I had surgery in 1961.
I had surgery in 1962.
I had surgery in 1963.
I had surgery in 1964.
I had surgery in 1967.
I had surgery in 1969.
I had surgery in 1973.

My body became the surgeons' practice field.

That first back operation in 1955 was for the removal
of the lowest disc in my spine and the fusion. This re-
sulted in fifteen per cent disability. It took over two
years for me to partially recover to the point where I
could do things fairly well. It was always a little bit
slower and a little harder for me to do what was normal. I
continued having difficulty for five years, until 1960.

In 1961 I had quite a lot of intestinal and abdominal surgery, and a hysterectomy. After recovering from this surgery I was feeling better than I had felt since before 1955. I was even working again.

THEN OUR CAR WAS HIT FROM BEHIND AGAIN, this time by another car! Back to the hospital again I went! This time I never even got to go home. They put me right back into the torture chamber for all the tests they had made before. But I praise God for doctors and hospitals. This time they found the second disc up from the bottom was ruptured, so in 1962 they operated — another laminectomy and spinal fusion. Since the accident, I had worn a neck brace because of a neck injury in the accident. It was a big collar around my neck that had one part resting on my chest and the other under my chin to hold my neck straight. It was most uncomfortable, especially in hot weather. From the time of the accident until the operation, I had to have traction on my neck, a ten-pound weight that made me feel like it was going to come through my brain. Praise God, after the neck operation, I didn't have to have traction any longer.

My neck kept giving me so much pain that in 1963 the doctors decided to make the spinal tests in the upper vertebrae. They found two discs out in the neck and arthritic-like spurs on them. This operation was done by opening my throat, taking out my larynx, my voice box, my esophagus and, as I understand it, laying it all out on the operating table. They went through the back of the neck and took out the two discs. This time they took bone from the front of my right hip to make the fusions. This meant I had bone taken from the front and back of my hip. They had to go rather deep into the hip. This made me feel like my hips were out of joint when I walked. The neck operation was not as painful as the lower back, but it hurt enough. They put a nail at the top of the spine to hold the fusion.

In the meantime, my lower back kept getting worse from the second accident, so in the spring of 1964 they operated again. This time they went through my abdomen and did what they call an anterior fusion. They actually fused one of the same discs that they had fused in the first operation, but this time they fused the front like they had the back before. In order to hold it properly, they put in a one and three-eighth inch screw at an angle.

In 1966 I fell over some reinforcing steel and again damaged my back. Back through the tests again and another operation in 1967. This time they could not fuse, but they did remove another disc. Because of the many operations, my heart and blood pressure began to show signs of trouble, so they just sewed me up without the fusion. Pain continued and seemed to get worse and worse, but I was resigned to endure it the best I could.

After the earlier operations, the doctors provided me with a canvas brace, first with light steel ribs in it, then after the second operation, with heavier steels over the light ones. But after this operation where no fusion was made, I had to wear a solid steel brace encased in leather. I could only take it off for short periods to relax or when it was extremely hot, and I removed it to sleep at night.

My husband, Wally, won a trip to Hawaii, including $200 spending money in December, 1968. Reluctantly the doctor permitted me to go since it was flying. He had restricted my travel to distances of under 100 miles by car. I wanted to say I stood in the Pacific Ocean so I walked out into the water and was thrilled until suddenly catastrophe struck!

An undertow caught me, swept me off my feet and with strain, struggle, and fright, the breakers finally rolled and tumbled me onto the beach. I felt like my whole back had been torn apart and I was not only hurting — I was scared!

Tragedy was confirmed when the medical examination later disclosed that all the rest of the movable discs of my entire spine had been ruptured. I was brokenhearted, our dream vacation had been tragically interrupted, we had a long, hard trip home, and my hope of ever being well vanished into darkness.

The confirmation of the damage had to wait until we got back home, but the distress of hopelessness and the pain, lessened to a bearable state by pain medication, was vividly present from the time of the tragedy until the doctor later told me the horrible news. I didn't want to go back to surgery so when we got back home, I started doctoring myself. But it seemed surgery had become a way of life for me.

By September, 1969, I could no longer stand the pain, so I went into the hospital for my sixth time through those terrifying, painful tests, and finally for my sixth spine operation. They removed the last two movable discs and fused them, plus fusing the one they couldn't fuse in 1967. By this time they had difficulty getting the bone for the fusions. They had already taken maximum bone from the front of my left hip and from my pelvic bone. They had cut under each knee to see if they could take the bone. My left leg was the one I could not walk on and they didn't want to mess up my good right leg. It took three surgeons five and a half hours to do the operation. They couldn't get my blood pressure up for quite awhile, so they couldn't give a hypo for all this time. Without the hypo, the pain was so intense that I just prayed to die. It hurt and it hurt and the hurt didn't stop with the surgery or the recovery time.

I stayed in pain from 1962 until 1973, and that's a long time to live with and in constant pain.

Recovery from this operation was extremely slow and difficult. I was in the hospital twenty-two days and couldn't even get out of bed alone. We had to have a hospital bed at home. I couldn't be out of bed at all unless I wore the steel, leather-encased brace. We had to have someone with me for four weeks until I could get out of bed by myself.

I really felt that life had pretty well come to an end for me. I didn't want to live any more because I was suffering so much, and it seemed as though I had no hope for improving. I didn't think I would ever be able to do anything again except just lie there — helpless and despondent. The doctors said I had a 100% disability.

I started having other sicknesses along with the back problems. People used to compliment me on how beautiful my hair was, but even my hair started falling out. I thought the medicine caused it. I didn't even bother going to a doctor for that. What was the use? Our doctor bills had destroyed all our financial hopes. I started wearing a wig in January of 1970.

By 1972 it seemed like everything in my body went wrong.

The potassium went down.

My kidneys malfunctioned.

My thyroid wasn't functioning properly.

I had something that had a long name that I can't remember.

My bladder was not working right.

Nothing in my body seemed to function right.

My hair eventually all came out except a few little bunches on the left side, and even that was rapidly falling out.

An internist said all my hair would fall out, even my eyebrows.

I think this was about the final blow!

My skin was flaking off in big white hunks and the doctors couldn't do a thing about it.

They had to even tell me I would never be any better. The only thing they could do was to give me pain pills and sleeping pills, along with other medication. They said this was to maintain me but offered me no hope for cure.

Finally in November of 1973 they operated on my bladder without going through the abdomen causing more scar tissue. The surgery was performed through the vaginal canal, causing my hips to feel like they were broken because of the lack of bones in them.

I WAS ABSOLUTELY SURE I WOULD NEVER WALK AGAIN!

I CAME HOME AND CRIED FOR A WEEK.

I just knew I would never be able to do anything again in all my life.

Since 1965, I had an income tax business so I could use my brain, even if most of my body was helpless. I wondered if I would ever be able to do that in the 1974 tax season.

I had someone make some long-handled forceps, tong-like things (like a barbecue tong) so I could pick up a paper clip or anything I dropped on the floor. Necessity made me find ways to do little jobs when my back wouldn't bend.

I had been taking two to four sleeping pills every night and pain pills every three to six or eight hours for over twelve years, ever since the second accident. That was a long, discouraging and agonizing twelve years, never without pain, never without medication, never free from going frequently to doctors. My hips used to go out of joint all the time with those bones gone. Friends used to try to cheer me up by saying you're so lucky that you don't have to scrub the floor. I could only reply, "You don't know what I would give to be able to scrub the floor." I could never describe to you the agony of the constant, never-ceasing pain night and day, day and night, time never seeming to pass and the pain never once leaving my aching body.

To go any place was no joy.

Christmas was an ordeal.

Going to church was terrible.

I was unhappy most of the time.

I forced a smile when I felt I had to, but there was no smile inside.

SOMETHING NEW IS ADDED!

Some friends of ours began to take us to some meetings called Charismatic meetings.

We began to hear talk about miracles and healings.

They talked about gifts of the Spirit.

We heard what they called messages in tongues and interpretations.

People talked about Jesus just like the Bible talked about him, only it was like he was alive today and still doing miracles, but now through people.

I didn't understand it, but we probably went to half a dozen meetings before December of 1973.

One day a friend said, "The Hunters are coming to town!" She seemed excited about this, but all I could say was, "Well, who are the Hunters?" She said they would be in Augsburg College in Minneapolis. It didn't make much difference to me who anybody was, because I was so hopelessly discouraged and sick. She said that the Hunters pray and God heals people in their meetings.

"How did you find out about all this," I asked.

She said she was on their mailing list and in their newsletter they list their schedule of speaking engagements and miracle services. She must have previously been to one of their services. She wanted to take me to the meeting but I was still confined to the house from the surgery. I felt nobody could ever do anything for me. I guess I wasn't thinking about the Lord at that time.

I said, "I'm too sick to go."

She said, "You're not doing any better here, so you might as well go. Just stay as long as you can and get prayed for."

Praise God for friends!

We decided to go in our car so we could leave if we didn't like it, or if I got too tired. I thought, "If I go and get prayed for and nothing happens, maybe they will leave me alone and quite bugging me to go to these meetings." So we went, more or less to get them off my back, not really even hoping for anything to happen to me. I just figured I was beyond hope! It was even too much for the Lord to do anything about. It's amazing how we can even forget that God can do anything!

We arrived early enough to get a seat about half way back. As the Hunters came in and I looked at all the people, I thought, "I'll never get near them anyway. What's the use of even praying."

The meeting began and all kinds of things began to happen that I hadn't seen before. Frances talked about how God had delivered her from five packs of cigarettes a day, instantly. She asked everyone who wanted to be delivered of any tobacco, drugs or alcohol to come forward for Jesus to deliver them.

Wally jumped up and went to the front for cigarette deliverance. When Charles and Frances laid hands on the heads of all those who went forward, they floated backwards to the floor. It was strange, because they seemed to barely touch them and instantly they fell backwards. Most of them didn't even bend; it was like they were stiff, but they looked relaxed. Some even fell backwards without anyone touching them.

Wally came back to his seat so excited! He said, "Oh, how great it was! I was slain in the Spirit!" He knew he had been instantly delivered. He knew Jesus had touched him and he was so excited he could hardly stop talking about it. As a matter of fact, he hasn't "come down" to earth yet after 3 years. It was about the greatest thing that ever happened to him. He was so mightily touched that people call him "Old Glory Face!" He likes that, because that's the way he feels.

My friend had bought a copy of the Hunters' book, SINCE JESUS PASSED BY, to acquaint me with a little of what might happen. They had described "slain in the Spirit, or falling under the power" in the book, so I knew about it, but this was the first time I had ever seen anything like it. I think it would have scared me if I hadn't read the book. The book also told some stories of people being healed, but this didn't seem to be possible for me.

I was curious about these people being "slain in the Spirit," so while Wally was up to be prayed for deliverance from cigarettes, before they started to pray for sick people, I got up and slowly edged my way up front where I could get a closer look to see if they were O.K. I couldn't see them good from where I was sitting. I felt like a dummy, but anyway I was curious enough to do it.

Then they began to pray for individuals. I got in the line but was jostled one way or the other and couldn't stay in the line. I was on the verge of crying. Tears began running down my cheeks. Finally an usher came over to me and said, "What's the matter? You are pale and look weak." I said, "This is my first time out of the house since I had surgery and I want to get prayed for but I can't even get in line." I had lost Wally in the crowd and couldn't find him or anyone else I knew. I must have felt like the sick man at the Bethesda Pool. He had been sick for thirty-eight years when Jesus asked him, "Would you like to get well?" "I can't," the sick man said, "for I have no one to help me into the pool at the movement of the water. While I am trying to get there, someone else always gets in ahead of me." (John 5:5-7 TLB). When I was jostled out of line and was getting so weak that I could hardly stand there, I felt like someone else was always beating me "into the pool at the movement of the water." I wish I had remembered that Jesus finally came along and healed him. All I could think of at the time was that someone else kept getting prayed for when I was edged out of the line. Everyone wanted so much to be healed that night. The healing waters seemed to be moving and people were being healed all over the front of the church.

The usher went over to Charles and whispered something to him, and Charles whispered something back to him. The man then came to me and took me to Charles for prayer.

I still felt that it was emotion that caused people to fall backwards, and I had good control of my emotions. I'm not sure I was even thinking about healing at the time. I was afraid that if I fell back I would hurt my back again, so I wasn't going to go down. He very gently touched me as he softly asked Jesus to touch me and heal my back. I had on snow boots that had half inch heels and I "dug" the heels into the carpet to brace myself.

I felt a power go into my head when he touched me and I took a little step backwards; then another step. I didn't know what was happening. Something was pushing me but I knew it wasn't Charles. He barely touched me. I ended up going down and found myself lying flat on the floor!

Wally had found me by that time and was next to me as I was under the power of God. I was aware of everything but the force of the power of God was like a "wind" of energy that pushed me back and held me to the floor. I began testing my hips first because they were so bad, and told Wally I still had some pain. When I got up by back didn't hurt! Charles prayed again for the pain in my hips. He also laid hands on both Wally and me and prayed for our marriage. Both of us went down again!

I had never been without pain in my hips since the 1962 surgery, and had never been free of the pain in the deep incision scar on my back where it was torn during so many operations.

When I got up this time I WAS FREE OF THAT AWFUL PAIN AT LAST!! IT WAS GONE!! IT DIDN'T HURT AT ALL!! IT DIDN'T HURT!! IT SEEMED SO IMPOSSIBLE, BUT GOD HAD DONE AN "IMPOSSIBLE MIRACLE!"

And it was so simple for him to do. I never realized before what a great physician Jesus is. He had performed an impossible surgery on me without testing, without pain, without anything except the gentle healing power of the Holy Spirit of God!

I went back to my seat and sat down. I FELT GOOD!

Much later that night I went to bed and I still felt good. I HAD BEEN HEALED AND I KNEW IT!

THE DEVIL PAYS A VISIT!

About noon the next day I began to have pain all over my body. But the one worst pain spot where it had hurt unceasingly for years didn't hurt! I KNEW I HAD BEEN HEALED! The hips were better, but again I had some pain.

I had read in SINCE JESUS PASSED BY how Satan will attack with symptoms to try to make you lose faith in your healing, so I was prepared for him. He really is deceiving, though. When you feel pain you can almost imagine more pain than you have. You can remember how bad it was before you were healed and you can so easily believe the devil's lies. I must admit that fear tried to attack my mind. I know the Bible tells me that fear is of the devil, but somehow, his negative salesmanship seems at the tempting time to be more positive and more practical than trusting Jesus. Isn't that stupid? God never tempts anyone! He will test us to make us stronger, but only the devil tempts. Can you imagine trusting Satan more than Jesus right after Jesus had taken years of pain out of your body? Just because some symptoms are put on you by the deceptive devil, you are tempted to believe Jesus isn't real and can't do miracles that will last.

It is so important that we (healthy or sick) constantly meditate on the promises of God in the Bible. Then when temptations come, and they will come to all of us, we have the knowledge of God's written promise that we can overcome any temptation the enemy can put in our path. Look at these three promises God gives to prepare us with the power of his word for just the time I was facing.

> Dear brothers, is your life full of difficulties and temptations? Then be happy, for when the way is rough, your patience has a chance to grow. So let it grow, and don't try to squirm out of your problems. For when your patience is finally in full bloom, then you will be ready for anything, strong in character, full and complete. (James 1:2-4 TLB)
>
> So be careful. If you are thinking, "Oh, I would never behave like that" — let this be a warning to you. For you too may fall into sin. But remember this — the wrong desires that come into your life aren't anything new and different. Many others have faced exactly the same problems before you. And no temptation is irresistible. You can trust God to keep the temptation from becoming so strong that you can't stand up against it, for he has promised this and will do what he says. He will show you how to escape temptation's power so that you can bear up patiently against it. (1 Cor. 10:12-13 TLB)
>
> Who his own self bare our sins in his own body on the tree, that we, being dead to sins, should live unto righteousness: by whose stripes ye were healed. (1 Peter 2:24 KJV)

JESUS HAD HEALED ME!

He gave me evidence that I was healed on Friday night!

I believed I was healed.

My body felt healed.

Jesus wants us to trust him so he can bless us.

When he said to Peter three times, do you love me, Peter? Do you really love me? He must have wanted so much for Peter to love him enough that when Satan's temptations came he would trust him, even when he was afraid he would lose his life. Peter failed Jesus and believed the lies of Satan that they would kill him. Peter needed power that he didn't have at his greatest time of temptation.

Was this my greatest time of temptation?

Would I, too, choose to believe the lies of the devil instead of the truth of God's promises? Would I deny Jesus thrice before the cock crew? Would I fall for his lies? Would I have more fear of the enemy killing me than trust that Jesus had healed me?

I had fear of being killed by the enemy, just like Peter had fear of being killed.

This was a very real fear to me.

My enemy was the painful, crippling, destroying diseases I had lived with for so long.

This fear was as real an enemy to me as Peter's enemies, and just as capable of killing me.

THERE'S ANOTHER PAIN!

Was that the one spot in my back on which I anchored my assurance that I was healed Friday night?

It was close to it.

No, it's not quite the same place.

Or, is it?

No, it's not really close at all.

I had discerned the devil's lie and I refused his temptation. God's assurance, his word which I had hidden in my heart, was my shield and my buckler!

> He that dwelleth in the secret place of the most High shall abide under the shadow of the Almighty. I will say of the Lord, He is my refuge and my fortress: my God; in him will I trust. Surely he shall deliver thee from the snare of the fowler, and from the noisome pestilence. He shall cover thee with his feathers, and under his wings shalt thou trust: his truth shall be thy shield and buckler. Thou shalt not be afraid for the terror by night; nor for the arrow that flieth by day; Nor for the pestilence that walketh in darkness; nor for the destruction that wasteth at noonday. (Psalm 91:1-6 KJV)

God had also made 1 Corinthians 10:13 real to me. You really can trust God to keep the temptation from becoming so strong that you can't stand up against it, for he HAS promised and will do what he says.

He WILL show you how to escape temptation's power so that you can bear up patiently against it.

He had done this just for me.

He had shown me that all the little pains and symptoms were not really to be feared.

He had shown me how to escape them.

God had kept his promise for me just like he said he would.

I didn't choose to trust the devil more than Jesus!

I didn't deny Jesus when he needed me to trust him!

Neither did Jesus deny me before my Father in heaven, because I didn't deny him. His love for me had become real enough that my love for him let me trust him.

I WAS TRULY HEALED!

Then the cock crowed!

PETER WEPT.

But I REJOICED!

Just as God had said, overcoming the temptation increased my faith — I became stronger in character so my destiny was to be full and complete instead of sick in defeat.

Jesus had healed each affliction I had been prayed for, but the Lord reminded me that I had not asked for healing of my illnesses other than my back, neck and hips. I guess I hadn't had enough courage or enough faith or enough guts or whatever it takes to ask them or to tell them about my hair problem and the causes of my hair all falling out. I was probably also embarrassed. God impressed on my mind to ask for everything to be healed.

We started at once to find out if the Hunters were still in the area. Wally spent the whole afternoon on Saturday inquiring and finally was told that they would be ministering at the Gospel Tabernacle on Sunday morning, the 9th of December.

We arrived at the church early and picked our seats the fourth row from the front. This time we had a lot more expectation than dread. God had beautifully demonstrated his mighty healing and delivering power in both our lives. The Hunters spoke that morning but had to leave early, so I had someone else pray for me — I don't know who they were, but I felt God was there to do the healing. I asked for and received prayer for a complete healing of all my defects and again was slain in the Spirit. After the prayer line was completed, they gave an invitation for those wanting to receive the baptism of the Holy Spirit. I responded and received and began praising God in a new language, just like they did in the Bible on the Day of Pentecost! Hallelujah. My life has never been the same since then. And I never had the pain again!

This new understanding of the healing power of God was a drastic change from the way I understood the teachings of my church. I was under the impression, apparently from my church teachings, that the Lord gives you ailments and illnesses according to your need for punishment. I presumed that, since I had been through so much pain and sickness for so long, I must have been very bad in God's sight. I didn't want to displease God, so I would try hard to live right, but assumed I wasn't doing very well because I thought God kept punishing me more and more. The harder I tried it seemed the more operations I had. I actually was afraid to go outside for fear God would strike at me again!

The thought never occurred to me to ever question this picture I had of the God of chastisement and punishment. I just accepted the assumption that I was bad and couldn't rise above that state. I later found out that I did need the extra power to rise above my state of being less than worthy in God's sight. It was the baptism with the Holy Spirit that gave me the power and the understanding of the true God in the Scriptures. I found out that it is the Holy Spirit who reveals the truth. The Bible took on a whole new meaning and a personal understanding of

the simple truth, and then I found God to be a loving and
personal God who wouldn't even think of imposing sickness or affliction on his children. People had told me that
God punished us with illnesses and in other ways just like
we punish our children. I didn't even stop to consider
that I wouldn't try to kill my children with some crippling punishment, nor break their bones or beat them
half to death just because they didn't obey me. It never
occurred to me that maybe God wouldn't be that mean
either!

Just before I went to the first Hunter meeting when
God began this fantastic series of healings, someone
among the Charismatic groups I had attended with my
friends said that sicknesses and afflictions came from the
devil. That was a completely new thought to me, and it
was hard to comprehend. Isn't it inconceivable that someone who had been exposed to the Bible and who thought
she was a Christian, would be so completely deceived by
the devil as to transfer the blame for sickness from the
devil to God? How could I have been so blind! Jesus
wasn't kidding when he called the devil a liar and de-
ceiver. He sure had me fooled for a long time. I KNOW
GOD DOESN'T CAUSE SICKNESS. It is the devil who
causes it, and God apparently allows him certain free-
doms, but praise God, he always wins by using all the
meanness of Satan to let his light shine brightly in con-
trast to the devil's darkness. I won the battle when God's
light was so brightly and tenderly shined on my inner life
for a healing even more important than the physical healings he gave me.

MORE MIRACLES!

My body was mightily touched by the power of God's Holy Spirit when Jesus, the great physician, healed me on December 8, 9, and 10, 1973. I went back to my doctor on December 18th, just a little over a week later. Even by this time, my hair was about an inch and a half long and was thick all over my head! When I first felt fuzz on my almost completely bald head, I was just a little afraid to be hopeful, but my hopes and faith were increasing. It didn't take God long to grow enough hair to convince me that he had hair-growing power as well as healing power. This was a thrilling time of my life to almost literally see the hair grow longer and longer.

Here is a letter my beauty operator wrote to tell of her part in watching God's Impossible Miracle in the making — while it was happening:

> "Being Norma Jean's beautician, I can truthfully say that her hair grew at an unusually fast rate.
>
> Its growth is approximately one inch per month, which is twice that of the average person's hair growth rate of only one-half inch per month.
>
> As far as texture is concerned, it seems to be thicker every time I do it.
>
> The Lord really knows how to bless abundantly!"
>
> Susan Cooke

The amazing part of this miracle was that as it got long enough to be shaped and tapered, it didn't need any changes! God let it grow perfectly styled and tapered, even better than a beauty operator could have done! I could hardly believe that God was doing such wonderful, personal things for me. How he must love us! It was impossible, but I could see it, and feel it! I give him all the glory and praise and honor for doing it for me. Can you imagine? For me who had mistrusted him so much for so long, he knew just what to do to bring to me, a mere human of no earthly importance, a perfect, personal miracle of such magnitude. To me, it was earthshaking and would have easily registered 10 on the Richter scale of the earthquakes of my imagination. The hair specialists could not believe how thick and how beautiful and perfect it was. They couldn't believe it was possible, but they saw it and admired it! Thank you Jesus.!! I love you, Jesus, for doing such a perfect miracle of my hair along with the fantastic miracles of my back, neck and internal organs, skin, heart and whatever else you healed when you made my body perfect! GLORY TO YOUR EVERLASTING NAME! I praise you, Jesus!

Jesus, I will do everything to live a life that will make you and God the happiest you can possibly be. With your power and help, I give you my whole life to use as you choose!

I went to an internist for examination. He believed in healing and didn't laugh at me. After his examination, he discharged me without any negative reports. The doctor who had done my bladder surgery also discharged me as being whole.

Charles had made a statement to me after he prayed the first time for my back. He said, "Don't throw away your crutches, braces, or medicine until you've checked with your doctor. Muscles get weak while wearing a brace so you need to let them get strengthened." I will always be so thankful for that because I had been wearing the steel brace since 1967 and my muscles were "shot." I didn't put on my brace on Saturday after my back was healed on Friday night and he was right — my back was weak. Had he not told me what he did, I would have been discouraged and probably my faith would have weakened, but I believed I was healed and accepted his statement that I would have to let my muscles strengthen before I could do entirely without the brace. Praise God for the gift of wisdom given him along with the gift of healing.

About the third or fourth of January, 1974, I went back to the doctor who was in charge of the back problems. He did not believe in healing and just laughed at me when I told him what had happened. I wanted him to give me a lighter, more comfortable brace, but he wouldn't let me have it. I had to wear the heavy steel brace which was encased in leather all through tax season. My muscles were so weak that I couldn't get along without something to support them. That brace was driving me nuts all through the hard work of the tax season. In July I went back to my back doctor, and insisted that I had to have a different kind of a brace. I felt like my back was healed and the brace was what was causing all the hurting. He reluctantly told me that he would write a prescription for whatever kind I wanted. He said I would always have to have the heavy steel brace, but because of my insistence, he wrote the prescription for a light brace with two steels for support. These could be removed as my muscles strengthened, which I fully believed would happen. It was my intention, and I told my doctor so he would be aware of what I planned to do, to first remove the two heavy steels in the brace and then later discard the whole brace. He said that I should not take the heavy steels out until January, 1975, at least, and I would have to wear the brace with the light steels the rest of my life. In September I removed the steels because my muscles had strengthened so much, and by the end of November of 1974 I was able to completely discard all support and left the brace off. Praise the Lord! What a relief!

I discontinued all medication at the end of the tax season of 1974. I had three medical tests made in the fall of 1974 and they showed all the skin condition problem and hair problems were completely gone, so the doctor officially stopped the medication (which I had already quit taking).

I waited about a year before writing to let the Hunters know about the healing, because I wanted to be sure I really was healed. I waited until I was completely out of braces and was sure nothing was coming back. Then I heard they were to be back at the Gospel Tabernacle in April of 1975, about seventeen months after they first asked Jesus to perform the miracles that changed Wally's and my entire physical, spiritual and mental lives. I was excited and was going to be able to tell them and show them personally what God had done! I would get to say those wonderful words, "I'VE BEEN HEALED!"

My hair had grown 13½ inches, and every hair was the same length, giving it that perfect beauty-parlor look, only even better than the best beauty operator could do. It was thick, beautiful jet black and always fresh looking and healthy!

I'm glad the Bible says that we can even call Jesus our friend, and he truly showed his wonderful friendship when he intervened in my behalf and healed me completely. No one will ever know, and I don't have the ability to express, how very grateful I am to him for his love, for his compassion and his personal touch to my body and my soul, and for his including my beloved Wally in his miracle-working, life-changing personal transformation of our whole way of life and purpose in living. All we both want to do now is to spend the rest of our lives for him!

I just can't begin to tell you how much different life is now. Wally could hardly realize what it was like to come home from work and find his meals prepared. It had been over twelve years since that had happened. He had been the one who had to add another job at the end of the day and take care of me year after year, day after day, night after night. He was the one who had to do the cleaning and other duties of taking care of our home.

Christmas, 1975, was different. It was an exciting day and I knew whose birthday we were celebrating. He was a very real person in my life and I knew he was not just a baby boy born of the virgin Mary; I knew he was the magnificent Son of God, Savior, Healer, and Controller of my life. I had fallen in love with this Jesus. He was real and alive in my life.

For all these years I had never been able to wear decent-looking shoes, if any at all. Now the flat shoes had been laid aside for whatever kind I wanted to wear. I have no more problem with my hips going out of joint. Everything we had done for all those miserable, joyless years was history. We had planned everything around a permanently disabled person until I was sick of it. Every plan we made, the clothes we bought, the food that was prepared by Wally or someone else, the constant trips to the doctors with the bills eating everything we could piece together and more — everything for a hopeless, crippled invalid.

BUT NOW IT'S ALL OVER! FOREVER! I'M WELL!

GLORY TO GOD FOR HIS MERCY AND KIND-NESS!

GOD'S MERCY SPILLS
OVER ON OUR MARRIAGE

Let me go back and share a little of what happened to Wally and what God did for him, and us together.

Wally had tried to be a Christian before all the sickness came into our lives, but no matter how you "try," you cannot live a Christian life on your own — it takes Jesus in you to do this, but we didn't know anything more than to try on our own, hoping we could be good enough to please God and get to heaven.

When the 1965 second accident hit and when our financial hopes were gone as we lost the lawsuit for damages, Wally lost all hope and all purpose for living. He just seemed to "quit" God and even stopped trying to live for him. Although he tried to hide it from me, he began accepting offers for beers and drinks from what he thought were friends. He hid his cigarettes from me, but I knew he was smoking. Even the guilt he at first had began to disappear as he got further and further away from the desire to be a Christian.

He grew colder and colder toward God and colder and colder toward me. As I complained to him about my pain, he became more grouchy and bitter about the situation. I can understand a little more how he felt now, but our lives became almost unbearable toward one another.

Our home had become a battleground for the civil war between us.

I would yell at him and he would come back at me with the same miserable attitude I had.

The sickness of our marriage was almost worse than the sickness in my body.

We were simply coexisting for economical reasons and necessity.

We couldn't afford financially to live apart — the bills took everything we had and we were deeply in debt and growing deeper.

Wally began to use foul language and cursing became more natural than decent words.

What was deep inside him began to flow out of his mouth with the vileness of the serpent he was serving, the very devil himself.

In July of 1973, Wally attended a Billy Graham Crusade and gave his life to Jesus. Deep in his heart he hated himself, but circumstances had pulled him into the control of the forces of evil. God kept drawing and drawing, but he couldn't yield his life totally to him.

Life for Wally was greatly improved, but with my sickness and pain and imposition on his time and pull against the life he wished he could have, he could not quit accepting the drinks from his "friends" and he could not give up the cigarettes he guiltily sneaked and hid around the house or in the car. Those unclean words kept flowing out of his mouth, telling what was on the inside. Trying to keep clean was like working in a garage with a white suit. His habits were dirty, but his heart kept wanting to be clean; clean enough for Jesus to live there. It was a different kind of guilt, but guilt it was and it hurt inside, and was hard to hide from people on the outside. It might be easier for Paul to explain to you what was going on inside Wally. Paul seemed to have about the same trouble. This is what he had to say about his striving to please God and self at the same time:

> The law is good, then, and the trouble is not there
> but with me, because I am sold into slavery with
> Sin as my owner.

I don't understand myself at all, for I really want to do what is right, but I can't. I do what I don't want to — what I hate. I know perfectly well that what I am doing is wrong, and my bad conscience proves that I agree with these laws I am breaking. But I can't help myself, because I'm no longer doing it. It is sin inside me that is stronger than I am that makes me do these evil things.

I know I am rotten through and through so far as my old sinful nature is concerned. No matter which way I turn I can't make myself do right. I want to but I can't. When I want to do good, I don't; and when I try not to do wrong, I do it anyway. Now if I am doing what I don't want to, it is plain where the trouble is: sin still has me in its evil grasp.

It seems to be a fact of life that when I want to do what is right, I inevitably do what is wrong. I love to do God's will so far as my new nature is concerned; but there is something else deep within me, in my lower nature, that is at war with my mind and wins the fight and makes me a slave to the sin that is still within me. In my mind I want to be God's willing servant but instead I find myself still enslaved to sin.

So you see how it is: my new life tells me to do right, but the old nature that is still inside me loves to sin. Oh, what a terrible predicament I'm in! Who will free me from my slavery to this deadly lower nature? Thank God! It has been done by Jesus Christ our Lord. He has set me free. (Romans 7:14-25)

What was missing? What did Paul discover that made the difference in his being able to turn away from the old evil nature inside him that held him in bondage? Wally wanted so much to be free, but in spite of all his earnest efforts, he just couldn't live like he knew he should and like he wanted so much to do.

Then came the night of December 7, 1973, when Wally and I went to our first miracle service. That night Frances invited all who wanted to be delivered from cigarettes to come forward. You can understand why Wally ran to the front of the auditorium to be delivered from this hold the devil still had on him. He meant it when he prayed with Frances Hunter for Jesus to deliver him from cigarettes. That's why he wouldn't stop rejoicing and talking about what had happened when he returned to his seat to tell me what it was like to be slain in the Spirit as Frances touched him. It was really Jesus who had touched him by the power of the Holy Spirit through Frances' hands as he fell backwards to the floor under the power of God never to be the same again. Then came the second touch in his life as a few minutes later, Charles laid hands on both of us and asked Jesus to bless our marriage. Charles didn't know how much we needed our marriage blessed. It not only needed blessing, it needed an overhaul as much as my body did. Both were hopelessly crippled beyond repair by any human power.

When Jesus delivered Wally that Friday night, he was completely and totally delivered of any desire for cigarettes, for beer or alcohol, and God cleaned up his mouth instantly. He has never had a desire or temptation since that night to smoke, drink or swear. This was done by the power of the Holy Spirit.

It was on Sunday morning that Wally went to Frances again and asked to be baptized with the Holy Spirit. Frances gently laid her hands on his head, he fell under the power of God and instantly began praising God and speaking in tongues, just like it happened in the Bible when Paul laid hands on the Christians.

This was the touch that changed Wally's defeat to victory in his Christian life. He had found what was missing. He found what Paul talked about in the eighth chapter of Romans when he moved from the defeat in his Christian life in the seventh chapter to the victory in the eighth chapter. Again, let Paul tell what happened to Wally when he received the baptism of the Holy Spirit.

So there is now no condemnation awaiting those who belong to Christ Jesus. For the power of the life-giving Spirit — and this power is mine through Christ Jesus — has freed me from the vicious circle of sin and death. We aren't saved from sin's grasp by knowing the commandments of God, because we can't and don't keep them, but God put into effect a different plan to save us. He sent his own Son in a human body like ours — except that ours are sinful — and destroyed sin's control over us by giving himself as a sacrifice for our sins. So now we can obey God's laws if we follow after the Holy Spirit and no longer obey the old evil nature within us.

Those who let themselves be controlled by their lower natures live only to please themselves, but those who follow after the Holy Spirit find themselves doing those things that please God. Following after the Holy Spirit leads to life and peace, but following after the old nature leads to death, because the old sinful nature within us is against God. It never did obey God's laws and it never will. That's why those who are still under the control of their old sinful selves, bent on following their old evil desires, can never please God.

But you are not like that. You are controlled by your new nature if you have the Spirit of God living in you. (And remember that if anyone doesn't have the Spirit of Christ living in him, he is not a Christian at all.) Yet, even though Christ lives within you, your body will die because of sin; but your spirit will live, for Christ has pardoned it. And if the Spirit of God, who raised up Jesus from the dead, lives in you, he will make your dying bodies live again after you die, by means of this same Holy Spirit living within you. (Romans 8:1-11)

It was the power of this same Holy Spirit living within Wally that gave him power to live above the desires to sin. Neither Wally or Norma Jean are perfect! But it was through the power Jesus promised to send back to us, the power that we were to receive when the Holy Spirit came upon us, that Wally and I were able to die to self and let Jesus truly be Lord of our lives, Lord and Deliverer from our old evil natures. That power of the Holy Spirit is still working within us to burn out the rest of our carnal nature, but the Holy Spirit living within us always gives us that ever-present desire to please God and Jesus in every act and thought. When a wrong attitude or thought tries to get into our minds, the Holy Spirit is instantly there to say "no," and we are quick to say "yes" to resist what Satan would like to do to pollute our minds and hearts.

Where Wally used to storm out of the house mad and grouchy, now he wakes up every morning with a peace and joy you wouldn't believe.

He drops on his knees to praise God and thank him.

He holds my hands before leaving for work and prays for me.

He returns home so full of the joy of Jesus that he can hardly wait to tell me all the things Jesus has done through him during the day.

He always asks Jesus to lead someone to him every day with whom he can share.

Almost every day he tells of some person in his work, or a child who has accepted Jesus as their Savior.

He can hardly stop talking about Jesus.

His life was turned upside down by this new-found power to witness.

His face shines with the glory of God night and day.

He loves Jesus so much that when he tells people what he has done for us and what he can do for them, tears flow out of his eyes. The tears of loving repentance run like rivers of water out of his eyes when he talks to God and Jesus like life-long friends. He can even talk to me for hours with a love for me like I never believed was possible. My love for him has been so magnified by the power of the Holy Spirit and the love of Jesus that our marriage is as near perfect as I could ever imagine.

They call him "OLD GLORY FACE" because he truly is filled with the glory of God night and day.

THE DEVIL STRIKES AGAIN!!!

It was seventeen months after my healing and our encounter with the Lord Jesus and the Holy Spirit through the Hunters that we walked into the church to meet them and share what had happened. They were asked to wait for us in the pastor's study. The pastor had just told them a lady and man would be in to share an exciting miracle that had happened when they were in his church before.

I walked in wearing high heel shoes and a full head of my own hair and a joy like no one could have on this earth without Jesus. They really didn't know what we were doing as I entered the room, bent over and touched my toes and then hugged them. With a back fused in so many places that it was impossible to bend at all, I was able to bend it with ease and touch my toes. I told them how I had helped Wally move furniture and do anything any normal, healthy woman could do. I had painted two of the bedrooms, ceilings as well as walls, which would have been impossible before. I had mowed and raked the yard, scrubbed the floor (and loved doing it), ridden a bicycle, driven the car, baked and cooked for lots of company, and anything else that came my way to do.

I told them about the day we had had an awful blizzard. We needed snow tires on both cars. Wally took the Duster and I drove the Olds. We spent five hours trying to make an eight block round trip. The Duster had two bald tires and he kept getting stuck. I wanted him to let me take the wheel while he got out to push, but the wind and snow was blowing so hard that it would just cut your face, so he wanted me to stay in the Olds. Without him knowing it, I got out of the car while he was gunning the Duster to get up a small incline and I pushed it out alone until he got up the grade. Can you imagine that! The muscles in my back had become as strong as a young woman's.

I tried to talk to Charles and Frances fast enough that night to piece together what I had been and what I now was by the healing, transforming power when Jesus touched me through them. They, of course, were thrilled to hear the story; and Wally and I hope it not only thrills you as you read it, but that it will bring hope not only for healing, but will bring faith to anyone who needs a healing. We pray that right now as you read this, the same power that raised Jesus from the dead and raised me from my bed of affliction will raise you from your sickness or affliction.

> "Jesus, thank you for your mighty healing power and for healing my body so completely. Jesus, we ask you to touch the body of the person reading this and heal them in the same complete, wonderful way you healed me. Thank you, Jesus, for the miracle of healing."

Several months after we shared with the Hunters about what God had done in our lives, they invited us to go to Houston, Texas and appear on their television program. We were delighted and it was a thrill to tell multitudes about what God had done. I was able to demonstrate the way I had once used that tong-like instrument to pick up paper clips or other dropped items when I couldn't bend my back. I showed that big steel brace and the lighter braces I had worn so long. Then I demonstrated how I could bend my back by touching my toes, running up steps and in other ways. I really never realized what an effect this testimony would have until months later they told what had happened to a man in California. They recorded the program on television tape to be sent around the United States and Canada and aired in different cities during the next several weeks. When it was played in one city in California, a man sat in his television room watching. He had had the same back problems I had, and had fusions just as my back had been fused. As he watched and heard my testimony his faith took hold and suddenly the power of God touched him and he jumped up, bent his back, began to jump and test it over and over again, and was completely and totally healed. He called the office of Hunter Ministries in Houston and was so excited telling them about this amazing miracle that he could hardly talk. God had used this television tape to record his miracle-working power and weeks later had spoken to the heart of a man hundreds of miles away to demonstrate the living Jesus.

Satan never likes to lose one of his potential victims. His deceiving ways and his counterfeit attempts to take away my healings were many and varied.

When we got back home from being on the television program, the devil made one of his attempts to make me think I would have more back troubles. Most people who have a back problem have something like a plywood board under their mattress. We had put a three-quarter inch plywood under our orthopedic mattress after my first operation. When we got home from Houston I started having backaches. Finally they got so bad I thought I couldn't stand it. I began to believe his lies, and to think it might be something more than his attempts to deceive me.

I began to wonder if the orthopedic mattress was getting soft or if I needed a harder mattress. I was trying to think of ways that might give me some relief. I asked Wally if he would take the board out and let me try it that way. It felt like feathers and I doubted if I would ever be able to sleep on it. I decided that my back couldn't hurt any worse and went ahead and used it that night. I thought if it was worse the next morning, we would have to get a harder mattress. I went to bed fully expecting not to sleep and probably not being able to get out of bed alone the next morning. To my surprise, I slept through the night and got up without a pain, and I have never had a pain since then. The board is now a shelf in our garage.

When I quit the last of my pain pills and sleeping pills, the devil tried to imitate the pain in my body and I took aspirin a few times. Finally he gave up and the pains ended. The first time I gave my testimony at church I was sick with pneumonia for three weeks. I didn't get the connection until I gave the testimony again, and got sick again. Then I realized he didn't want me to talk about what God had done. He tried to convince me that if I didn't shut up, I would be sick again. When he found out I would tell my story anyway, he started making me sick before I would speak. It had to be Satan, because the first time I didn't get sick was when the pastor asked me without telling me beforehand, and the devil didn't have time to make me sick.

I began speaking out of town at meetings and because I knew the dates in advance, I would get sick each time. The attacks were worse and lasted longer. One time a cold went down into my chest and I suffered with a terrible coughing spell. It seemed he even tried to keep me away from my own church so I couldn't be prayed for. I think the last attack like this happened just before I was to speak in Alexandria, Minnesota. I got what I call the "plague." I coughed so much that I vomited. I don't think I ever coughed so much and so hard in my life. I went anyway, but I stopped by the church and my pastor rebuked Satan, bound him and his power, and asked Jesus to heal me. I wasn't sick even a minute more after he prayed. We had the best meeting that day we had ever had.

I thought the devil had given up the battle, but months later Wally and I had the exciting privilege of taking a boat cruise from Miami to Nassau with the Hunters on a

Delightfully Charismatic Christian Walk Seminar. The devil tried in several ways to block us from getting there, but he didn't succeed and the day arrived when we were on the ship and were being fed the word of God by the practical teachings of the Hunters. We were having the thrill of our lives. We were asked to go to the deck to have group pictures made. The photographer began positioning us for the picture. He asked us to move back a step. I didn't notice a four-inch ledge and when I stepped back I lost my balance as my foot dropped off the ledge, fell backwards and in an attempt to catch myself, I turned sideways and fell further over a three-foot ledge and landed across a deck chair. My rib hit the arm of the chair with such an impact that I thought I had torn my whole back apart.

I knew I was badly hurt, but the sudden fear that struck me was even worse. I just knew that I had torn my back apart and the thoughts that I would be right back where I was those long, horrible years of torture rushed to my mind. I cried from the pain and the fear. Wally was almost in shock with fear. Charles and Frances rushed to me while others were also trying to help. They immediately took spiritual authority over the devil and his powers and commanded my body to be healed and commanded the spirit of fear to leave. The pain subsided a little, but was still hurting. My side began swelling and in a few hours I had two big bruises in the shape of hearts on my hips. The swelling was rather bad and caused additional pain. After much prayer, most of the pain left about ten o'clock that night. By the next morning the swelling had gone down by my rib and I could move the rib and hear it crunch and I knew it was broken.

I went to the ship's doctor and he made arrangements for me to have it X-rayed when we docked at Dodge Island in Miami, Florida. The doctor examined me, felt the rib as Wally and I told him how it crunched and he said he could feel it too. He and the nurse both said it was broken. The nurse got me into a gown and put me on the X-ray table. While she put the film in, or whatever they do, I said, "O.K., Lord, do your thing and do it quickly!" That was all the time I had to pray. They took an X-ray. The doctor looked at it and felt my rib again.

He took the X-ray again, and again looked at it and felt my rib.

He took a third X-ray and again looked at it and felt my rib. I could tell that each time he felt it, it didn't move or crunch and I had felt it and it wasn't like it was before. I began to praise God and thank him for healing it. The doctor said he knew it was broken but his X-ray equipment wasn't as strong as it was in the hospital, so he sent me to a hospital in Coral Gables. Before I left, the ship's doctor showed me the X-ray where the mark was that should have been a break, but it didn't show a fracture. I said, "Praise the Lord!"

We went to the hospital in Coral Gables where another X-ray was taken and another doctor examined me. They took them a second time. A mark was on the X-ray, but it was not a fracture. They said it was just a bruise and dismissed me. Obviously the Lord healed it before the nurse could snap the X-ray picture at the doctor's office on Dodge Island. We praised the Lord for the healing and for making the rest of our vacation trip what it was. Had the rib been broken, it would have ended our trip. I would have had a difficult time riding over 1,500 miles back home in an automobile. God wouldn't let the devil have his way and ruin this trip, even though he really tried.

This was just another confirmation that my back had been made totally new and strong, because the previous damages in ruptures of the vertabrae were caused by less than this accident. God is a good God! Hallelujah!

I can't even wonder or imagine what life would be like, if I had life left, had my friends not insisted that I go to that first meeting. I don't want to even think about it. Life is too glorious like it is, and Wally and I look forward to the exciting things Jesus is going to do with each new day.

I know Charles and Frances didn't do these miracles. I know God did them through the Lord Jesus Christ, and to him we give all the glory and praise.

> So for the second time they called in the man who had been blind and told him, "Give the glory to God, not to Jesus, for we know Jesus is an evil person."
>
> "I don't know whether he is good or bad," the man replied, "but I know this: I WAS BLIND, AND NOW I SEE!" (John 9:24-25)

Neither I nor the doctors can explain what Jesus did to my back and neck. After the fusions the doctors and I know that I could not bend my back, and now we all know that I can bend it freely.

I don't know how he did it, "but I know this:

I COULDN'T BEND, BUT NOW I CAN!"

Authors' Note:

As a part of the verification of these remarkable miracles in Norma Jean, we asked her to have a doctor in Minneapolis examine the records which were available and to X-ray her spine to let us know certain facts we felt would be of interest to the readers of this book, as well as to exalt Jesus in the performance of these miracles.

A doctor told Norma Jean before she had the X-rays made in August, 1976, that if the fusions were shown to be properly holding and the screw and nail were still in place, the greatest miracle would be that she could bend her back as freely as she did in high school. Her back previously wouldn't and couldn't bend with the fusions in place.

We are including her doctor's letter.

17 Dove Lane, North Oaks
St. Paul, Minnesota 55110
August 27th, 1976

Mr. Charles Hunter
10420 Memorial Drive
Houston, Texas   77024   re: Mrs. Norma Jean Van Dell

Dear Mr. Hunter,

As you know, Mrs. Van Dell asked me to examine the medical
records which you mailed up from Houston, Texas; as well as the
X-Rays of the Lumbo-Sacral Spine, taken at Unity Hospital, Fridley,
Minnesota on Aug. 25th, 1976 and interpreted by Dr. Harry Mixer,
Radiologist. I also examined Mrs. Van Dell.

I will first answer your specific questions as relayed to
Mrs. Van Dell in your telephone conversation with her.

1. You asked, "Is the 1 3/8" screw still present"? Ans.:
Yes, the 1 3/8" screw which was inserted during her operation of
March 18th, 1964, is still clearly evident and is firmly in place.
Please find enclosed Dr. Mixer's report. You will note in his
report that the screw still transfixes the lumbosacral joint and
I would therefore conclude that this operation has been most successful.

2. You asked, "are the fusions from the previous operations
still present?" Ans.: Yes, You will note again in Dr. Mixer's
report, that the extensive fusions from the previous surgery are
also clearly evident on both sides, from the 4th Lumbar Vertebra
and extending downward into the sacrum. This too, confirms the
success of the previous surgery.

3. You asked, "Are the donor sites for the bone removed from
the pelvic bones still visible or have they all healed in?" Ans.:
The donor sites are clearly visible as translucent areas in the
Iliac Crests on both sides, indicating the donor sites from which
cortical cancellous bone grafts were taken. Although Dr. Mixer
doesn't mention these in his report, they are mentioned by another
Radiologist as incidental findings on films of the abdomen which
had been taken about a year previously. I compared these films and
they are practically identical.

On physical examination, Mrs. Van Dell's back has a quite
good range of motion. On forward flexion, she can't quite touch
the floor, stopping short by about 3 or 4 inches. This is about
average for many people in her age range. The multiple surgical
scars are readily apparent, but I elicited no significant pain
when palpating the area. Mrs. Van Dell stated that prior to her
healing, she used a large quantity of pain-relieving medication, as
well as sleeping pills etc. on a regular basis. But since then,
none are needed.

- 2 -

In the September, 1976 issue of CHRISTIAN LIFE magazine, Charles Farah, Jr, has contributed an article entitled: "Toward a Theology of Healing". In this article, he states, "God heals through doctors and God heals through prayer. All true healing is divine, whether God does it through natural means, doctors, or through supernatural means. God wills to heal".

Francis MacNutt, O.P., in his book, HEALING, (1974 by Ave Maria Press), states on page 274: "Sometimes God works through nature and the skill of doctors; sometimes he works directly through prayer and sometimes through both, but always there should be co-operation, mutual respect and an admiration for the variety of ways in which God manifests his glory."

I find myself in agreement with the views as expressed by these two men of God.

In summary then, in my opinion, Mrs. Van Dell has experienced at least two kinds of healing:

1. God's healing through her doctors (skilled orthopedic surgeons, a neuro surgeon etc.). whose operations appear to have been successful. Repeated surgery was necessitated after repeated accidents and recurrent trauma.

2. Supernatural healing with relief of her pain and because of this, increased freedom of movement and an ever-widening range of activities, including riding a motor cycle!

3. She probably also experienced a supernatural Inner Healing which freed her of anxiety and much apprehension and many fears. This has enabled her to venture out and constantly expand her range of activities and interests. I believe the healing will continue as she commits to the Lord, more and more of her past feelings of resentments, bitterness etc.

Mrs. Van Dell because of her accidents and many operations, has experienced a great deal of suffering, both physical and mental as well as emotional.

When we observe her present-day busy schedule, carried out in a cheerful attitude and with a most optimistic outlook, we can't help but rejoice with her in her miraculous recovery. For all of this we give thanks and praise to our Lord and Savior, Jesus Christ!

Sincerely in Him,

Myles E. Estlund, M.D.

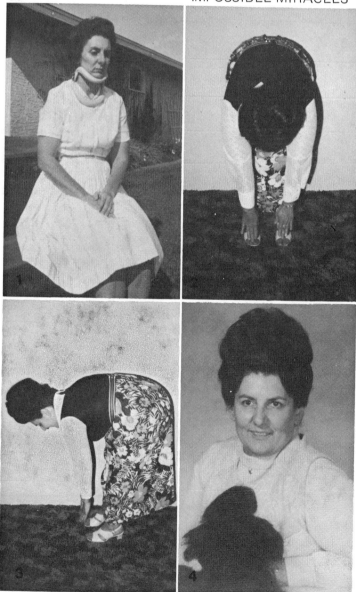

1 After visit to hospital in 1962.
2/3 August, 1976, showing flexibility of back
4 Norma Jean Van Dell, formerly bald, holding sack of hair which was trimmed from her head about 20 months after miraculous back and hair healing!

GOD'S MIRACLE FOR EILEEN

by Eileen Swanson

THE OLD HOUSE

What is that pain that keeps hitting my spine? Probably the weather. No, there it goes again, but this time it really is making my shoulder blade hurt! I wonder if there's something wrong with me? It couldn't be, or could it?

By 1960 I was convinced that there was something really wrong because the pain in my spine and shoulder blade area was becoming more and more pronounced as I performed my household tasks. I went to our family physician and he prescribed a high-potency vitamin B which I took for almost two years, but the pain still continued.

In 1962 it had progressed to the point where I could not reach up over my head with both arms to hang up clothes.

I had always been a "scrubber" in my house, and I loved to wash windows, but washing windows was becoming very painful and while I liked to wash them on the outside at least twice during the winter months, I had to stop because of the pain.

Suddenly the pain hit my chest as well as the spine! Our family physician had left the medical practice to become a psychiatrist in the fall of 1963, so in the meantime I tried treatments with an osteopath which gave temporary relief, but the pain would come back again within a few hours. Even if I walked on the beach in 80° weather without a sweater, the wind would cause severe pain.

I decided to see an orthopedic surgeon at the urging of my family and friends because whatever I had, kept getting more and more widespread and more and more painful. He took X-rays and prescribed a muscle relaxant. He also suggested that I be under the care of an internist, and in an attempt to relieve the almost constant pain he sent me to the curative workshop for deep-heat treatments and whirlpool therapy. I did this and then attempted an exercise program at home. The pain increased in the spine when I did some of the exercises, so I discontinued them.

In 1964 while my husband was deer hunting, I awoke early in the morning with extreme pain in my arm. I had a habit of sleeping with one arm over my head and the pain was almost unbearable, and the arm was frozen, or locked, in an over-the-head position! I tried to call out to our sons sleeping in another room, but the pain was so intense I couldn't get much more than a loud whisper out. Not only was the pain in my arm, but it had spread to the chest area as well.

As soon as the doctor arrived in his office I called him and explained what had happened and about the pain I was having in my spine and chest. It certainly was obvious in my voice. He explained that he thought it was fibromyositis, and I was given a prescription for muscle relaxants.

In December of 1964 I was again sent to the curative workshop for treatments, this time by an internist. The treatments didn't seem to be helping me. I would look at all these people who were so crippled and here I was a healthy-looking woman. I think I felt out of place, but the doctor explained that no matter what I looked like on the outside this pain was real and I KNEW it!

I was very much aware of the pain I had day and night and it was becoming worse! I was now aware of pain in everything I did.

Even a simple little thing like letter writing was painful.

Wiping up floors was painful.

Making beds was painful.

Holding packages was painful when I went to a store.

Talking on the telephone was painful and unpleasant because of holding the receiver!

Running the vacuum was painful.

Washing dishes was painful.

Cooking was painful.

Sitting down was painful.

Getting up was painful.

Lying down was painful.

Standing up was painful.

Everything was painful.

I could not continue with any task because once the pain started, it would increase the rest of the day unless I completely stopped doing anything. I soon learned to taper off and not do much in any one day. Even in spite of medication, my spine was still very painful.

In March of 1965, the doctor sent me to the hospital for X-rays of my spine. After he examined the X-rays he told me I had osteoarthritis of the spine with deterioration and that I would have to learn to live with pain as there was no cure as yet for this disease. I was stunned — I was dazed — I don't remember what I said to him. I just remember I didn't know what arthritis was, much less osteoarthritis, but it was something painful, THIS MUCH I KNEW! When he said there was no known cure, I thought of the pain and the years ahead of me, and I was only 38 years old. My world fell apart!

When the doctor told me I had osteoarthritis and that I would forever have to live with the pain, and that it would in all probability get worse and worse, I cried out to God for help! I knew he knew how I felt! I had never known anyone who had been healed by God, and had only heard about a man named Oral Roberts who had people healed as he prayed. This really didn't register any hope for my healing, but I had read God's word and it said that Jesus could heal people. I didn't know how God could do anything about my hopeless condition, but I knew if anyone could, it would have to be God. If he didn't do something, then there was no hope.

I looked up the word "osteoarthritis." The medical definition is "degenerative joint disease." The definition of degenerative joint disease is, "A chronic joint disease characterized pathologically by degeneration of articular cartilage and hypertrophy of bone, clinically by pain on activity which subsides with rest; it occurs more commonly in older people, affecting the weight-bearing joints and the distal interphalangeal joints of the fingers, there are no systemic symptoms." (Blakiston's Pocket Medical Dictionary, McGraw-Hill Book Company)

I didn't understand it, but I didn't like it.

The doctor gave me a shot of novocaine and then a shot of cortisone in the spine to counteract the pain. I felt fairly good on Saturday, but by Sunday morning I had pain all over my entire body where it hadn't been before. The shots were really a forewarning of what was to come. He discontinued them and gave me instructions to rest and not put my arms over my head for fear they would lock in that position and cause extreme pain.

Then I went into depression. I cried for no reason at all. I was tired all the time! It seemed I never got over being tired. I was tired when I went to bed. I was tired when I woke up. I was tired all the time. My doctor explained to me that it was the pain that was causing the fatigue. I hadn't even realized this. I'm not the kind who likes to lie down and rest during the day because I have so many things to do. Not only that, if I did try and lie down, all the work I had to do would keep running through my mind and I couldn't rest at all.

When my children were small and taking afternoon naps, I would sit down and read the Bible and thoroughly enjoy it, but as they grew older, I grew away from this wonderful habit, and know now this was a big mistake.

In 1965 when this terrible depression hit me, I began attending Monday night Bible studies, and while I enjoyed them, my daily Bible reading was still cast aside. It seemed like I had so many things to do. The depression was so heavy, I cried most of the time and felt that no one in the entire world loved me. Even though my children would come and put their arms around me I couldn't seem to stop. Still that feeling continued that nobody loved me.

NOBODY LOVES ME! What a horrible thought, and yet I couldn't stop this feeling. Deep within me I knew God loved me, so one night when I was feeling particularly miserable I picked up my Bible and just sat there and held it in my lap. I didn't open it or read it. I just held it.

The next night I picked it up again, I opened it and started to read. A change came over me that I can't explain, but somehow I KNEW things were going to be different. I knew God loved me and cared about me and so did my family! Instantly the depression left!

The depression was gone, but the household tasks became harder to do, the pain more severe and the tired feeling more exhausting. I'd go to bed with pain and wake up with pain, and along with this, that terrible feeling of constant exhaustion. I was tired of being tired!

Then I went to an eye, ear and nose physician, because in addition to being tired I was having terrible pain in my head, face and jaw. I could hear the jaw joints as I opened my mouth to eat. He said it was arthritis of the jaw bone which caused the pain.

On May 19, 1967, my doctor sent me to The Green Bay Orthopedic Company with a prescription for a steel back brace. By this time my back kept wanting to curve in, especially when I would sit for any length of time during church services or in the car. Driving was very painful, but I had learned to hold the wheel at the bottom and steer, rather than raise my arms as you normally would do. This helped.

I went to the Orthopedic Company and was fitted for the brace. I was stunned as I stood there and realized that there was no way I could bend in this brace. I thought of all the things this would keep me from doing. I had them take the brace off and tearfully told the man I just wasn't ready for something like that yet. I became determined that this disease wasn't going to conquer me. I was going to challenge it all the way. I knew God would give me strength because he was doing this daily. I knew if I wore the brace I would get too stiff from not bending at all. I was already having big problems with stiffness and I could see that being in a brace would really cause me to get worse. He showed me a less expensive one — a shoulder support. This I used when we would go on a trip. It helped my shoulders and spine.

In the meantime the doctor gave me prescriptions for the arthritis, but I couldn't tolerate the medication for any length of time because of the reaction on my stomach.

By 1968 the arthritis pains had continued to increase in my spine and neck-shoulder area as well as the chest. At night I would be awakened out of a sound sleep with sharp pains across my chest. I remember the first time it happened I thought I was having a heart attack and was going to die right then and there. It happened so many times I finally got used to it. Sometimes the cold weather would cause the same reaction. I got to the point I didn't even want to go out in the cold!

One Sunday I had muscle spasms and a lot of pain in the neck area, and as I was standing in line to take communion, I suddenly passed out from the intense pain. I wondered how much more I could stand.

I had had continuous pain in my entire mouth from one jaw joint to the other for over a year, plus the pains in my ears. I was sent to an orthodonist to be sure it was not a dental problem. He made a cast of my bite and found that to be okay. I was then sent to an internist who made 5 X-rays of the jaw joint. He also made a rheumatoid test, but found no rheumatoid arthritis.

By 1970 my hips were increasingly painful and stiff. Getting in and out of the car or a chair, bending over to pick something up or to take something out of the oven made me feel as if someone had inserted a rod across my hips so I couldn't straighten up.

By 1974 the pain in my left arm became so severe that I couldn't sleep on it at night. The minute I would turn on my side, the pain would wake me up. It hurt from my shoulder to my elbow. My physician sent me to Bellin Hospital in April, 1974, for NCV3 (nerve ending tests).

They stuck needles into my arm.

They stuck needles in my hand.

They stuck needles in the fleshy part of my thumb.

They stuck needles into the ends of my fingers.

They stuck needles in the back of my shoulders.

The machine would register the findings wherever the needles were placed and then the doctors told me the awful news: muscle atrophy.

No cure.

No hope.

No medication.

No therapy.

My elbows were so painful I couldn't lift a bowl of vegetables, much less a skillet from the stove to pour the gravy. The boys would do it for me. I had real difficulty trying to do dishes, so my family would also have to do this for me.

We have a two-story colonial home with washing facilities in the basement, so I had to do a lot of stair climbing. I found a little relief by going down the stairs backward, but finally my knees and hips couldn't take it any more.

My husband and I talked it over and decided to sell our home and look for one with everything on one level. In May of 1974 he contacted a realtor and explained our problem. I prayed and asked the Lord to lead us to the right home for us because I knew God knew how much pain I was having. Every home he showed us was too small. Our furniture wouldn't fit in it. We looked at several, and my heart cried out, "Oh, Lord, you know how much pain I'm having. Please lead us to the home you know will be the one we need." But no home we looked at would do. The yard was either too small or something else wasn't right and I became discouraged, but somehow I knew God wouldn't let me down. My body was the temple of God spiritually, but it was a dilapidated home physically.

Which way should I turn?

Which way could I turn?

MY NEW HOME

The Lord had another plan for us! Praise his Holy Name!

He answers prayer, but in a much different way than we expect sometimes! He answered mine in a much better way, because instead of a one-story house, he made a change in my body, his temple, instead of my home.

It happened a little after 10 P.M. on the night of July 13, 1974! Here's how!

Several women had been meeting for lunch where we thanked God before and praised him after eating. This had become a highlight in my life and was filling a deep hunger for more of God. I had been reading books written by Charles and Frances Hunter and loved their exciting relationship with Jesus and the thrilling way they had of portraying the joy and victory in serving him. I thought I had read all of their books, but apparently I hadn't. I didn't know what had really happened because I didn't know they had written a book called THE TWO SIDES OF A COIN. And then I discovered they were going to be speaking at one of these luncheons.

The Hunters shared with exciting enthusiasm what Jesus was doing and I loved every word. They were talking of things I hadn't read in their books. Things like miracles that had been happening in their services. I didn't really know what to think, but somehow I believed what they were saying was true. Their books had always been real and alive to me.

After they spoke they invited all those who wanted to receive the baptism of the Holy Spirit to go to the back of the room. Someone had also said something about being "slain in the Spirit." All this was strange to me and I didn't understand what it all meant. Even though it sounded different, it seemed that they had something I wanted in my life. This one thing I knew — if God had a gift for me, I WANTED IT! I don't know what happened, but when Frances touched me I floated backwards to the floor and it was beautiful.

They spoke with such assurance about the healing power of Jesus that I was filled with awe! They told stories of healings that happened in their meetings that were so much like those of the New Testament that it was like they were telling Bible stories, but I knew they were current events. Then they talked about the miracle service at the high school auditorium that night. They said Jesus was going to pass by and would be healing the sick. They talked about what would be happening that night with such conviction that I had no doubt that there would be healings. I was so excited that I could hardly wait for the time for the service to arrive.

We got to the auditorium almost an hour early so we wouldn't miss a thing. I had pain in every joint in my body that night.

At this time I was Chairman of the Green Bay, Wisconsin arthritis group and served on the board of directors of the Arthritis Foundation of Wisconsin. I had a deep, personal interest in people with arthritis and wanted to do all I could to help them.

The miracle service began with a lot of praising God and I loved it. I was really spiritually fed that night.

Up to this time I had a knowledge from the word of God that people could be healed, but so far as I knew I had not yet been able to believe in my heart that I would be healed. The way they talked that afternoon caused me to know in my mind, but the reality that I would be healed had not fully reached my heart. I wanted to be, and I had hopes. What would it take to change this from head knowledge to believing in my heart?

When the miracle service got under way something was happening within me. Right after the singing started I could feel the power and the presence of Jesus. When we were worshipping God in song, they began to sing in languages that I didn't know. They later said this was called singing in the Spirit. It was beautiful, but even more, I could feel the power of God like I had never felt it before. The Bible says that tongues are for the unbeliever. When I heard singing in tongues, it caused me to believe in speaking in tongues and in power.

I had never seen the Lord worshipped and loved so much in my entire life. Even if I had not been healed I would still have remembered the miracle service because of the love and adoration of the Lord! My life really changed.

Then the Hunters had everyone in the audience stand real straight with our feet together and extend our arms forward. They were asking God to heal backs. With our arms stretched forward, palms together, they asked God to do the miracle of healing backs and letting arms grow out. A lady from our Bible study group was standing next to me and was healed! I watched her arm grow right out until they were both the same length. She is able to do all kinds of things now that she couldn't do before. This was the very first miracle I had ever watched God do and it was beautiful! Glory!

People all over the auditorium had their arms grow out at the same time. It was real exciting and you could just see and feel the power of God at work in the meeting. It was like Jesus had come there in person that night and was doing his miracles right in front of us.

Then they began announcing over the microphone that people were being healed in the audience, and as they called out first one disease or affliction and then another, the people would respond by going to the microphone and telling what God had just done for them. I could hardly believe what was happening. I wondered how they knew about the healings, but they spoke with authority and the testimonies of the people who were healed were exciting and genuine.

At different times during the service, Frances came to the front of the stage and announced, "A woman with arthritis and deterioration of the spine" — and that is all she said. She didn't say "Come forward," or "You've just been healed." That was all she said. Three different times she said this. I thought, "Oh, Lord, that's me!" But I was aware of how many people in Green Bay had this condition. I worked with so very many who were afflicted with it.

Then they talked about marriages. They asked couples to stand and then they had them say their marriage vows again. The service was nearing the end. We who were married were all standing by our seats when Frances' attention was drawn to a woman in the front row. Frances and Charles left the stage and approached her and I heard them say, "Arthritis and deterioration of the spine," and then I knew she was the one they had been talking about during the service. I can't tell you how happy I was for her. I knew what her life was going to be like without all that pain day and night! WOW! My attention was focused on her and I didn't want to miss seeing her healed and slain in the Spirit. As I stood there so filled with joy for her, in my mind I said, "Hallelujah, Lord!" Just as I said that I was slain in the Spirit and fell back into my seat!

My daughter said, "Mom's healed!"

A friend who was two seats down from us said to his wife who was sitting next to me, "Eileen's fainted!"

I was so awed by it all that I was speechless.

The people around me just looked. They, too, were awed by my being slain in the Spirit as I just stood there by my seat because no one touched me.

My back hit that wooden back on the seat and it left a red mark which my husband found the next morning, but I felt no pain! I felt nothing at all except a nice, warm feeling in the spot that had been deteriorated!

Before I ever got up, I KNEW I HAD BEEN HEALED!

Before the healing, when we were riding in the car and my husband would brake suddenly, the jar would cause the arthritis pain to go the whole length of my spine and then I was in trouble for the rest of that day and usually the next day. But, praise God, even after the hard fall against the back of the wooden seat, I HAD NO PAIN! The next morning I HAD NO PAIN. HALLELUJAH!!!

My whole body was healed in that instant when the power of the Holy Spirit touched me.

My back was healed!

My neck was healed!

My shoulders were healed!

My elbows were healed!

My hips were healed!

My knees were healed!

My spine was healed from top to bottom!

My mind was healed and my spirit was healed. My whole life has been transformed by the touch of Jesus! Now I didn't need a one-story house because I could run up and down the stairs.

Later that night, I received the baptism of the Holy Spirit, and even the power in my life changed. This has added a dimension to my life and a power that enables me to boldly tell of the love of Jesus and to be the witness Jesus said the power would give. Thank you, Jesus, for the gift of the Holy Spirit!

Our youngest son, Jim, said, when I told him of my healing, that he thought it was "neat," but at first he didn't believe it. Then he said, "I saw for myself that you were healed. Then I believed."

Dave said, "I don't think you should have any more X-rays taken, you have had enough of them. Now that you are healed, people will see that you are healed without you having to prove it to them."

AND SEE IT THEY DID!

I am spreading the Good News far and wide and constantly that Jesus healed me and they see me as a living, active, strong, energetic, totally-healed person.

> Don't worry about anything; instead, pray about everything; tell God your needs and don't forget to thank him for his answers. (Phil. 4:6)

FATHER, I THANK YOU WITH ALL OF MY HEART FOR THE MIRACLE YOU DID FOR ME — THE IMPOSSIBLE MIRACLE!

Eileen Swanson reflects great joy in healing!

WIRETAPPING

by T.K. — Easton, Maryland

I fell out of a tree and crushed a vertebra twenty-three years ago!

Little did I know then what would happen to me as a result of this during the next eighteen years. This back injury took me through six major operations during the eighteen years. I went from doctor to doctor, from hospital to hospital, and from pain to continuous excruciating pain, as they operated in New York, Washington, Minnesota and New Jersey.

The words from the doctor almost paralyzed my mind. He indicated that I had two choices: an operation the first of June which might leave me paralyzed; or postponement of the operation and a temporary delay of the paralysis. He felt that I would be paralyzed by September anyway. I thought, "What's the difference whether I'm paralyzed in June or September." I didn't want to be paralyzed at all. Sometimes we are inclined to blame our doctor for problems he had nothing to do with. Too often we also blame God for things Satan throws at us. Satan causes sicknesses and just because God in his complete wisdom doesn't stop what the devil causes, we blame God.

From a surgical standpoint, the operation was successfully performed. They removed another disc and fused my spine. This was a total of five discs that had been removed and fusions made. They also put a stabilizing wire along my spine. They rerouted all the nerves to take the pressure off. With all they could do for me, the pain continued and continued and continued until . . . .

I went to a home prayer meeting one night at the home of Graham and Treena Kerr. Charles and Frances Hunter were their guests that night. So many people came that we had the meeting outside on their beautiful lawn overlooking the waterfront. At the end of the meeting they began to pray for the sick or other needs of the people who were there. It was amazing to see people fall back to the ground as Graham and Treena and Charles and Frances just touched them. They had talked about healings and said people would be healed that night as Jesus touched them. I could see things happening and could hear people talking about being healed. Then Charles came up to me to pray.

He asked me what I would like Jesus to do for me.

I didn't tell him very much, but said I had a bad back problem. Truthfully, I didn't know whether to have him pray or not. I was afraid I might not be healed. I was also a little afraid that I would fall under the power like the rest of the people and I didn't know about that. I knew that my back wouldn't bend.

. Charles just touched my back with his hand and said, "Jesus, heal him."

I felt a warmth go into my back and I floated backwards to the ground.

I lay there flat on my back for what seemed to me to be about fifteen minutes. My back felt like it was on fire. I knew something was happening. I could feel the power of God upon me. I didn't want to do anything that would interfere with whatever it was that God was doing, and I knew he was doing something.

Finally I sat up.

I SAT UP!!!

But I couldn't sit up!

My spine was bending, but it couldn't bend!

THAT WAS IMPOSSIBLE!

With the fusions and the wire, it just couldn't bend.

Something had happened!

I stood up, bent my back, touched my toes, twisted my back and did everything I could to test it, and it was working perfectly. AND THERE WAS NO PAIN! IT WAS AS FREE AS IF NOTHING HAD EVER BEEN WRONG WITH IT. GOD HAD DONE A MIRACLE! MY BACK HAD BEEN HEALED!

I later went back for a checkup to the hospital where my last operation was performed. They made the necessary examination and X-rays and then told me their findings.

I HAD FIVE NEW DISCS IN MY SPINE AND

THEY DIDN'T EVEN FIND THE WIRE!

PRAISE GOD FOR HIS PERFECT WIRETAPPING JOB!

WHAT IS A MIRACLE?

by Frances

Mr. Webster has this to say about a miracle: "In theology, an event or effect that apparently contradicts known scientific laws and is hence thought to be due to supernatural causes, especially to an act of God. A wonder or wonderful thing."

And that's the way we feel about miracles. Every miracle whether it is large or small, contradicts known scientific laws and therefore must be due to supernatural causes, especially to an act of God. And isn't a miracle a truly wonderful thing!

Sometimes we put miracles into just one category, that of healing, and yet there are impossible miracles happening all around us, and waiting to happen around us, if we will just call upon the supernatural power of God to help us. Too many times we call an impossible miracle a "coincidence," or "luck." These words should never be in a Christian's vocabulary, because if we're trusting in God, let's give him the glory for whatever happens in our lives!

We love these "impossibles" that happened to us recently. We were flying to the east coast one day and I had been having trouble with contacts. I discovered a long time ago that it's impossible for me to ever use cream on

my face because I never manage to get every smidgin of it
off and when I put my contacts in, the cream gets on the
contact and causes a film to form which is the most
difficult thing in the world to get off. And the bad part
of not getting it off is that I can't see through my contacts when they're fogged up with cream, and my vision
is absolutely zero.

I had been struggling all the way to Atlanta on the
plane, trying to "blink" off the cream, and in spite of
prayer, using eye drops and everything I could think of,
nothing worked! One eye was fair, but the other eye had
nothing but a big blur! Charles held my arm as we
changed planes in Atlanta and guided me around ob-
stacles and finally we boarded the big L-10 that was to
take us to our final destination.

When we got on the plane, I was really praying that
God would clear up the lens when all of a sudden I
realized that the reason I wasn't seeing was because the
lens had come out, apparently somewhere along the line
as I had rubbed my eyes trying to remove the film. I
almost panicked, because this would mean a ten-day trip
without sight in one eye.

Bob, our son-in-law, immediately said, "I'll go back in
the airport and ask God to show me right where it is!!"
We all really prayed up a storm! When Bob told the
stewardess why he was getting off, she said, "You'll never
find it!" Bob prayed all the way out to the lobby where
we had been standing, asking Jesus to show it to him, and
it was as though a beam of light was directed to the spot
where it fell out, and there it was, waiting for him to pick
it up!

A situation that contradicted known scientific laws?
Yes, because how could you ever find a tiny contact in an
airport the size of the Atlanta airport? What would your
"chances" be of not having it destroyed by some 200 or
more people stepping on it as they boarded the L-10?
What scientific law would ever state that a contact could
be missed by that many feet all stepping in the same
small area?

A wonder? Yes!

A wonderful thing? Yes!

An impossible miracle? Yes, except for God!

The other night we were talking to a friend of ours who mentioned that he had lost his class ring during the day. We asked him if he was sure he had it on when he left the house that morning to go to work. He was confident he had it on and yet somehow there was a word of knowledge that it was in his house. We asked him if he had looked all over his house, and he said he had. Then we prayed and said, "Jesus, will you direct him right to the place where that ring is and let him see an impossible miracle!"

We finished our telephone conversation, hung up, and within two or three minutes, we got a call right back, and he was excitedly yelling on the other end of the telephone, "I found it, I FOUND IT!" Jesus had directed him to his tennis racket, and as he opened the cover, he discovered his ring safely nestled there, waiting for him to discover his impossible miracle! Isn't God good?

Last year in one of our crusades, God used his beautiful sense of humor to speak to a man in one of our services. During one of our "cigarette deliverance" times when I asked the cigarette smokers to come forward, he said to himself, "I've smoked for 40 years, and I'm not about to give it up now, and I'm sure not going to go up there," so he didn't come up. Then I made a call for men in the audience to act as "catchers," because most people fall under the power of God in that moment of yieldedness when they are willing to give up something that has become a strong part of their life. This man said to himself, "Well, that won't hurt me, I'll go up and catch." What a shock he got when he discovered that the power of God had gone through the person he caught and had moved into him, and he was instantly delivered of 40 years of smoking! Hallelujah!

An impossible miracle? Yes, for those who don't believe in the supernatural power of God, but who can believe in God without believing in his supernatural power? The entire Bible is supernatural, and so is God, and so is Jesus! Salvation is supernatural, praise God! So is the baptism with the Holy Spirit! Hallelujah! So is eternal life! All of these contradict known scientific laws, but praise the Lord, they're real!

One of the most supernatural things that ever happened to me occurred during my water baptism. My life was absolutely revolutionized by this "glory" moment in my life. Charles and I had wanted for a long time to have a water baptismal service so that those who had never had the privilege of sharing in this beautiful command in the Bible, "repent and be baptized," would be able to know the reality of water baptism. We tried renting a motel swimming pool, but God held our hand. After watching a service in our church, we asked our pastor if he would like to join with us in a mass water baptismal service. He said he would put his staff to work immediately to look for a suitable lake for the event, but we all wished it could be a river.

AND THEN GOD MOVED!!! Evangelistic Temple the very next week received 65 acres of land, just 25 miles north of Houston, worth possibly $1,000,000 and debt free, as a GIFT! Bordering the property is the sandy-beached San Jacinto River which we temporarily re-named the "San Jordan" River.

We announced the mass water baptismal service on our television programs, sent thousands of letters across the United States and prayed asking Jesus to baptize people with the Holy Spirit when they came up out of the water, and to wash their diseases away in the river.

They came, by the hundreds, walking down a dusty road, carrying loaves of fishes and bread, following after Jesus . . . . . Some were old, some young, some black, some white, some with entire families, some seemingly alone, and yet part of a throbbing exciting group of Christians who had gathered on the banks of the San Jacinto River in southern Texas, for one purpose — to be obedient to the word of God and submit to water baptism. It was a scene that could have taken place two thousand years ago. The dresses were a little different, but the fervor was the same as the eunuch had when he asked Philip, "Look! Water! Why can't I be baptized?" "You can," Philip answered, "if you believe with all your heart." And the eunuch replied, "I believe that Jesus Christ is the Son of God!" He stopped the chariot, and they went down into the water and Philip baptized him." (Acts 8:36-37.)

And they believed with all their hearts! More than two thousand people of all denominations lined the banks of the "San Jordan" River to participate in an old-fashioned river baptism. They came from Visalia, California; Baltimore, Maryland; Atlanta, Georgia; Niagara Falls, New York; Louisiana; Missouri; all over the state of Texas. One woman vacationing here from Holland, got caught up in the excitement and came to be baptized.

They came walking down that dusty road together all in one accord: "Water baptism is what I want!" There were Methodists, Catholics, Lutherans, Presbyterians, Episcopalians, Baptists, Assembly of God, Nazarenes, Church of God, 1st Christian, Pentecostals, Free Methodists, Salvation Army, Friends and people who had no church affiliation, but who wanted to participate in a great "Glory" day for the Lord!

Somehow or other, I didn't see the beautiful sleek air-conditioned cars parked in orderly rows by the Harris County Sheriff's Dept. they had just left. All I saw was people who loved Jesus just as much as those disciples did who trudged down a dusty road after him some 2,000 years ago. They were singing as they walked along, and even though shuttle busses had been provided, people seemed to feel there was something special about walking the quarter mile down to the baptismal site. They were carrying picnic baskets of all sizes and shapes and there was a festiveness to the air, and great anticipation. There were those who had been confined to wheelchairs who came, believing their ailments would be washed down the river upon baptism. There were socially prominent people . . . people of great wealth . . . unknowns . . . ex-alcoholics . . . people from poverty row . . . all loving Jesus the same way. There were children in bathing suits, ladies in pants suits of all kinds, long maxi dresses of all descriptions, but the same love of Jesus in the eyes of every single one of them. Men were dressed in their church clothes, beach clothes, work clothes . . . all walking with the same enthusiasm . . . there was a judge there, excitedly taking pictures of everything he could see, completely carried away with the excitement of the day!

There were chicken dinners and hot dogs, soda pop and sand, but everyone was so interested in the baptism they lost interest quickly in the food. Everyone was talking about Jesus, and how they heard about the baptismal service and what they were expecting. Television cameras were whirring, movie cameras of all descriptions were panning the scene, and yet nobody wanted to "perform." They were all willing to let God film what he wanted recorded of the occasion. Two scuba boats with "frogmen" patrolled the scene to prevent any accidents.

Then there was singing. It started with "Give Me That Old Time Religion" and the voices swelled to earbreaking proportions as more than two thousand people joined in the singing. Everyone was clapping to the beat as they were singing, and the sounds carried up and down the river as "Jesus Joy" broke out all over the entire meeting. Like Zacchaeus, who was too small to see what was going on, a little blonde boy climbed up one of the willow trees lining the bank and watched the entire service from that vantage point. "It was good for Paul and Silas, and it's good enough for me!" seemed to echo everyone's thoughts there. Then it was "I Love Him Better Every Day!", "Down by the River Side," "Oh, How I Love Jesus," "Hallelujah" and a few more, and soon the men who had been chosen to do the baptizing walked down into the river, two by two, and took their places up and down the river in the roped-off areas.

Charles walked into the water to meet and join with the pastor of our church, Austin Wilkerson, who was sitting in a boat, waiting to give a message on water baptism. When he finished, he slipped over the side of the boat into the water, shoes, socks, tie and all, and the first baptismal candidate walked out. The first one was a new Christian of just a few months, but with a zeal to put most mature Christians to shame. Then she heard the question, "Have you accepted Jesus Christ as your Savior and Lord?" Her "yes" was loud enough to be heard by the entire gathering. She didn't want anyone to have any doubt about this big moment in her life. Then the Pastor said, "Upon the confession of your faith in Jesus Christ as your Savior and Lord, I baptize you into the death, burial and resurrection of Jesus Christ, in the name of the Father, the Son Jesus, and the Holy Spirit." And under she went! She came up beaming all over, praising God, a brand new creature in Christ! The fact that her wig had come off and was starting to float down the river didn't faze her at all! Someone grabbed it and handed it to me and said, "Praise the Lord for wigs!" She was lost to this world because the Shekinah glory of God had fallen on her and the things of the world had grown strangely dim.

As soon as their names were checked off, the candidates were helped into the water and down to the persons who were baptizing them. There were 8 baptizing groups and each had been instructed to let everyone have an experience in water baptism that they would never forget. We had instructed the group that those who wanted to receive the baptism with the Holy Spirit at the same time could expect this, and as soon as they came up out of the water, to raise their hands and begin praising God. Many received before they went under the water because of a complete and total surrendering of themselves to God. The San "Jordan" River almost became a salt water river because of the tears that flowed. Whole families went in together to be baptized at the same time. One of the most beautiful sights was a negro family with 6 children who walked out together to follow Jesus in baptism. Married couples of all ages walked out hand in hand to be baptized into a perfect union with Christ, as they went under the water together.

They crowded the shoreline, pressing to get in. I had the beautiful privilege of shaking hands with each person as they entered the water and giving a special greeting to each one. The power and presence of God became almost overwhelming as lives were changed as they went under the water and came up "new creatures in Christ!" Their old selves had been buried with Christ by baptism. Hallelujah!!! Glory!!! Praise you Jesus!!! could be heard all over the place. They came out of the water and were grabbed by their families and friends and tears splashed all over the place. Many times during the baptismal service, the presence of God became so overpowering that people went under the power before they were immersed and had to be helped back to the beach. One woman had come all the way from California because God had spoken to her and said she needed to be baptized in the river, and the glory of God so fell on her that as she came out of the river, two men had to catch her as she went under the power. They laid her gently down on the sandy beach, and for two hours God did a supernatural work in her life as she was "slain in the Spirit" this entire time, never to be the same again!

Some of the most dignified, sophisticated Presbyterians and Methodists I know were lost in the beauty of the moment and forgot the mud that had seeped up through the sand by the time they got down to the beach. Shoes were left at the edge of the river by people who even forgot they had come with shoes on because of their "glory" hour. The enthusiasm became contagious, and suddenly there was a rush of people who had come to be spectators but who had been caught up in the holiness of the hour, and decided this was their day for baptism, too.

They walked into the water with some of the most beautiful dresses and hair-dos I've ever seen, and they could have cared less what happened to them because God was speaking to their hearts, and who can resist the call of God when it becomes like a drum beating inside your chest? One woman had on a beautiful long dress which billowed out like a huge balloon as she walked into the water looking right straight up into the face of Jesus!

The sun beat down, but no one seemed to mind the heat. The path up the hill was getting muddy from all the wet feet and clothes, but nobody seemed to mind because everyone was looking up, and not down. There were sunburned bald heads, but nobody seemed to mind. There were moments when there was a holy hush and people seemed unable to speak because of what had just happened to them.

A Catholic man in a wheelchair who had just been saved that day, decided he wanted to go in, wheelchair and all, and down the ramp they took him. They turned the wheelchair around backwards in the water, and after his confession of faith, he was baptized by tilting the wheelchair backwards. They brought him out of the water and up the hill again. He sat on the top of the hill with his paralyzed body stiff as a board. I walked over to him and said, "In the name of Jesus of Nazareth, WALK!" He looked at me questioningly. I simply said, "It's been done!" He said, "It has?" I said, "There was enough power surrounding you when you were baptized (6 men had carried him) to let 10 men walk."

I walked over and sat down for the first time all afternoon. I LOOKED UP AND HE WAS WALKING!!! There was a small shout throughout the crowd, but no one actually seemed surprised. They just BELIEVED it was going to happen, and it did! I talked to his wife who said he had a stroke three and a half years ago and hadn't been out of the wheelchair since that time. Praise God for his healing power so apparent in today's world!

Laymen who had never participated in baptismal services before walked around almost dazed after it was over because of what it had done to their lives. People were rejoicing because of the numbers who came out of the water baptized with the Holy Spirit!

People began walking the road back to their air-conditioned cars. Again it seemed nobody wanted to ride. They just wanted to be alone with God at this very special time. We saw some of the baptizing pastors eating their chicken dinners as they walked back down the road to their cars. There were drooping hair-dos and drippy clothes, but no one seemed to mind — they were thinking of the things in the spiritual world!

A few stayed on, most returned to the church for the evening Praise Celebration, but some got so happy they could hardly contain themselves. Joan said she'd never forget those who came in wheelchairs being carried into the water to be baptized; Bob said the thing that impressed him was the expression on the face of the people who were spectators and who cried and rejoiced and praised right along with those who were being baptized.

As for Charles and me, all we could see were people, "walking down a dusty road, carrying loaves of fishes and bread, following after Jesus!"

An impossible miracle? Yes, to everyone but God! Who would believe in a day of air-conditioning and modern conveniences that people would go to all that trouble just to be baptized? We would, because we were there.

WHY MIRACLES?

by Charles

God created the world by a miracle!

God created man by a miracle!

God loves the man he created by a miracle and has used miracles ever since to draw men unto himself.

God could have used force to bring his created being into heaven and into a heavenly relationship with him, but God chose to do it a different way. He chose to offer all mankind the opportunity to love and serve him, and the entire Bible is devoted to God's patient efforts to win man to his mighty love. It is hard to realize that any one of us would choose to pull away from the mighty love that God wants to give us, but that's the way God planned it.

One of the most interesting studies I have ever made in the Bible was on the subject of miracles as we were writing this book. As I systematically went through the Bible I discovered there were many, many reasons for God's miracle-working power, from creation to destruction. Look at the reasons for God's miracles!

Ex. 3:19-20: "But I know that the king of Egypt will not let you go except under heavy pressure. So I will give him all the pressure he needs! <u>I will destroy Egypt with my miracles</u> and then at last he let you go . . . "

WHY MIRACLES? — TO DESTROY OUR ENEMIES

Ex. 4:29-31: So Moses and Aaron returned to Egypt and summoned the elders of the people of Israel to a council meeting. Aaron told them what Jehovah had said to Moses, and Moses performed the miracles as they watched. <u>Then the elders believed that God had sent them</u>, . . .

TO CAUSE BELIEF

Ex. 6:6-9: "Therefore tell the descendants of Israel that I will use my mighty power and <u>perform great miracles to deliver them from slavery, and make them free</u> . . ."

TO FREE FROM ENEMY — SIN

Acts 7:36: ". . . And <u>by means of many remarkable miracles he led them out of Egypt</u> and through the Red Sea, and back and forth through the wilderness for forty years . . ."

TO DELIVER FROM SLAVERY — SIN

Ex. 10:1: Then the Lord said to Moses, "Go back again and make your demand upon Pharaoh; but I have hardened him and his officials, so that <u>I can do more miracles demonstrating my power</u> . . ."

TO DEMONSTRATE GOD'S POWER

Ex. 13:3: Then Moses said to the people, "This is a day to remember forever — the day of leaving Egypt and your slavery; for <u>the Lord has brought you out with mighty miracles</u> . . ."

TO REMIND HIS PEOPLE OF THEIR DELIVERANCE

Ex. 13:14: "And in the future, when your children ask you, 'What is this all about?' you shall tell them, '<u>With mighty miracles Jehovah brought us out of Egypt from our slavery</u>' . . ."

TO KNOW OUR REDEMPTION FROM SIN

Ex. 14:31: When the people of Israel saw the mighty miracle the Lord had done for them against the Egyptians, they were afraid and revered the Lord, and believed in him and in his servant Moses.

MIRACLES BROUGHT FEAR AND RESPECT FOR GOD

Ex. 34:10-11: The Lord replied, "All right, this is the contract I am going to make with you. I will do miracles such as have never been done before anywhere in all the earth, and all the people of Israel shall see the power of the Lord — the terrible power I will display through you. Your part of the agreement is to obey all of my commandments; . . . ."

TO DISPLAY POWER THROUGH PEOPLE

Num. 16:30: ". . . But if the Lord does a miracle and the ground opens up and swallows them and everything that belongs to them, and they go down alive into Sheol, then you will know that these men have despised the Lord."

TO IDENTIFY THOSE WHO DESPISED GOD (SINNED)

Num. 14:10, 11: But the only response of the people was to talk of stoning them. Then the glory of the Lord appeared, and the Lord said to Moses, "How long will these people despise me? Will they never believe me, even after all the miracles I have done among them? . . ."

TO CAUSE THEM TO BELIEVE GOD

Num. 14:20-23: Then the Lord said, "All right, I will pardon them as you have requested. But I vow by my own name that just as it is true that all the earth shall be filled with the glory of the Lord, so it is true that not one of the men who has seen my glory and the miracles I did both in Egypt and in the wilderness — and ten times refused to trust me and obey me — shall even see the land I promised to this people's ancestors . . ."

TO SHOW THE IMPORTANCE OF MIRACLES AND OF OBEDIENCE

Deu. 1:28-29: '... They have even seen giants there — the descendants of the Anakim!' "But I said to them, 'Don't be afraid! The Lord God is your leader, and he will fight for you with his mighty miracles, just as you saw him do in Egypt. And you know how he has cared for you again and again here in the wilderness, just as a father cares for his child!' But nothing I said did any good. "They refused to believe the Lord our God who had led them all the way, and had selected the best places for them to camp, and had guided them by a pillar of fire at night and a pillar of cloud during the day ..."

WHY MIRACLES — TO LET US KNOW GOD WILL FIGHT FOR US WITH MIRACLES

Deu. 4:9: "But watch out! Be very careful never to forget what you have seen God doing for you. May his miracles have a deep and permanent effect upon your lives! .."

TO SHOW IMPORTANCE GOD PLACES ON MIRACLES

Deu. 4:32-35: "... An entire nation heard the voice of God speaking to it from fire, as you did, and lived! Where else will you ever find another example of God's removing a nation from its slavery by sending terrible plagues, mighty miracles, war, and terror? Yet that is what the Lord your God did for you in Egypt, right before your very eyes. He did these things so you would realize that Jehovah is God, and that there is no one else like him ..."

SO WE WOULD REALIZE THAT JEHOVAH IS GOD AND THAT THERE IS NO ONE ELSE LIKE HIM!

Deu. 7:8: "... It was just because he loves you, and because he kept his promise to your ancestors. That is why he brought you out of slavery in Egypt with such amazing power and mighty miracles. .."

JUST BECAUSE HE LOVES YOU

Deu. 7:19: ". . . Do you remember the terrors the Lord sent upon them — your parents saw it with their own eyes — and the mighty miracles and wonders, and the power and strength of Almighty God which he used to bring you out of Egypt? Well, the Lord your God will use this same might against the people you fear. . ."

WHY MIRACLES — GOD WILL USE MIRACLES AGAINST THOSE YOU FEAR

Deu. 11:7: "But you have seen these mighty miracles! How carefully, then, you should obey these commandments I am going to give you today, so that you may have the strength to go in and possess the land you are about to enter . . ."

TO GIVE FAITH-STRENGTH TO GO TO HEAVEN

Judges 2:10-11: But finally all that generation died; and the next generation did not worship Jehovah as their God, and did not care about the mighty miracles he had done for Israel. They did many things which the Lord had expressly forbidden, including the worshiping of heathen gods.

TO CAUSE CONTINUING WORSHIP OF GOD

Psm. 75:1: How we thank you, Lord! Your mighty miracles give proof that you care.

TO GIVE PROOF THAT GOD CARES

Psm. 86:8-10: Where among the heathen gods is there a god like you? Where are their miracles? All the nations — and you made each one — will come and bow before you, Lord, and praise your great and holy name. For you are great, and do great miracles. You alone are God.

TO DISTINGUISH THE ONE GOD FROM OTHER GODS

Psm. 95:8: Don't harden your hearts as Israel did in the wilderness at Meribah and Massah. For there your fathers doubted me, though they had seen so many of my miracles before.

TO SUPPORT GOD'S PROOF OF HIS DIETY

Psm. 111:3: For his miracles demonstrate his honor, majesty, and eternal goodness.

WHY MIRACLES — TO DEMONSTRATE GOD'S SUPREME POSITION

Isa. 55:13: Where once were thorns, fir trees will grow; where briars grew, the myrtle trees will sprout up. This miracle will make the Lord's name very great and be an everlasting sign of God's power and love.

TO PROVIDE AN EVERLASTING SIGN OF GOD'S POWER AND LOVE

Dan. 4:3: It was incredible — a mighty miracle! And now I know for sure that his kingdom is everlasting; he reigns forever and ever.

TO PROVE THAT THE KINGDOM OF GOD IS EVERLASTING

Matt. 11:4: Jesus told them, "Go back to John and tell him about the miracles you've seen me do ... 'Blessed are those who don't doubt me.'"

TO PROVE THAT JESUS WAS GOD'S SON

Matt. 11:22-23: "... Truly, Tyre and Sidon will be better off on the Judgment Day than you! And Capernaum, though highly honored, shall go down to hell! For if the marvelous miracles I did in you had been done in Sodom, it would still be here today."

TO SHOW SERIOUSNESS OF DOUBTING JESUS WHEN MIRACLES HAVE BEEN DONE

Mark 5:27: She had heard all about the wonderful miracles Jesus did, and that is why she came up behind him through the crowd and touched his clothes.

TO INSTILL FAITH BY MIRACLES

Mark 9:39: "Don't forbid him!" Jesus said. "For no one doing miracles in my name will quickly turn against me ..."

TO SHOW SECURITY IN MIRACLES

Mark 16:20: And the disciples went everywhere preaching, and the Lord was with them and <u>confirmed what they said by the miracles that followed their messages.</u>

WHY MIRACLES — TO CONFIRM WHAT THEY SAID

Luke 4:25: For example, remember how Elijah the prophet used a miracle to help the widow of Zarephath — a foreigner from the land of Sidon. There were many Jewish widows needing help in those days of famine, for there had been no rain for three and one-half years, and hunger stalked the land; yet Elijah was not sent to them.

TO HELP A WIDOW

John 2:11: This miracle at Cana in Galilee was Jesus' first public demonstration of his heaven-sent power. And his disciples believed that he really was the Messiah.

TO PROVE THAT JESUS WAS THE MESSIAH

John 2:18-19: "What right have you to order them out?" the Jewish leaders demanded. <u>"If you have this authority from God, show us a miracle to prove it."</u> "All right," Jesus replied, <u>"this is the miracle I will do for you:</u> Destroy this sanctuary and in three days I will raise it up!"

TO SHOW THE AUTHENTICITY OF JESUS' DEATH AND RESURRECTION — THE REDEEMING MIRACLE OF ALL AGES.

John 2:23: <u>Because of the miracles</u> he did in Jerusalem at the Passover celebration, <u>many people were convinced that he was indeed the Messiah.</u>

TO SHOW THAT IT WAS THE MIRACLES WHICH CONVINCED MANY THAT HE WAS THE MESSIAH

John 3:1-2: After dark one night a Jewish religious leader named Nicodemus, a member of the sect of the Pharisees, came for an interview with Jesus.

"Sir," he said, "we all know that God has sent you to teach us. Your miracles are proof enough of this."

WHY MIRACLES — TO SHOW PROOF THAT JESUS CAME FROM GOD

John 4:45: But the Galileans welcomed him with open arms, for they had been in Jerusalem at the Passover celebration and had seen some of his miracles.

TO CAUSE THEM TO WELCOME JESUS AND ACCEPT HIM

John 5:20: ". . . For the Father loves the Son, and tells him everything he is doing; and the Son will do far more awesome miracles than this man's healing."

TO SHOW PROOF THAT GOD LOVES JESUS

John 7:31: Many among the crowds at the Temple believed him. "After all," they said, "what miracles do you expect the Messiah to do that this man hasn't done?"

TO PROVE THAT HE WAS THE MESSIAH

John 10:24-25: ". . . . If you are the Messiah, tell us plainly." "I have already told you, and you don't believe me," Jesus replied. "The proof is in the miracles I do in the name of my Father . . ."

TO PROVE THAT HE WAS THE MESSIAH

John 10:32: Jesus said, "At God's direction I have done many a miracle to help the people. For which one are you killing me?"

TO HELP THE PEOPLE

John 10:41-42: ". . . John didn't do miracles," they remarked to one another, "but all his predictions concerning this man have come true." And many came to the decision that he was the Messiah.

TO FULFILL PROPHECY

John 14:11: ". . . Just believe it — that I am in the Father and the Father is in me. Or else believe it because of the mighty miracles you have seen me do."

TO PROVE THE ONENESS OF THE FATHER AND SON

John 14:12-14: "In solemn truth I tell you, anyone believing in me shall do the same miracles I have done, and even greater ones, because I am going to be with the Father. You can ask him for anything, using my name, and I will do it, for this will bring praise to the Father because of what I, the Son, will do for you. Yes, ask anything, using my name, and I will do it! . . ."

WHY MIRACLES — TO BRING PRAISE TO THE FATHER

John 15:24: ". . . . If I hadn't done such mighty miracles among them they would not be counted guilty. . . ."

TO SHOW THAT IF WE DON'T BELIEVE WITH MIRACLES WE WILL BE COUNTED GUILTY AT JUDGMENT

John 20:30-31: Jesus' disciples saw him do many other miracles besides the ones told about in this book, but these are recorded so that you will believe that he is the Messiah, the Son of God, and that believing in him you will have life.

WHY MIRACLES — THE MOST IMPORTANT REASON FOR MIRACLES IS PROOF THAT JESUS IS THE MESSIAH

Acts 2:22: "O men of Israel, listen! God publicly endorsed Jesus of Nazareth by doing tremendous miracles through him, as you well know . . ."

MIRACLES WERE GOD'S PERSONAL ENDORSEMENT OF JESUS AS THE MESSIAH

Acts 8:6: Crowds listened intently to what he had to say because of the miracles he did.

MIRACLES CAUSED PEOPLE TO LISTEN TO THE GOOD NEWS PREACHED

Acts 14:3: Nevertheless, they stayed there a long time, preaching boldly, and the Lord proved their message was from him by giving them power to do great miracles.

TO PROVE PREACHING WAS FROM GOD

Romans 15:19: I have won them by my message and by the good way I have lived before them, and by the miracles done through me as signs from

God — all by the Holy Spirit's power.

PAUL WON GENTILES PARTIALLY BY SIGNS FROM GOD

1 Cor. 10:3-4: And by a miracle God sent them food to eat and water to drink there in the desert; they drank the water that Christ gave them. He was there with them as a mighty Rock of spiritual refreshment. Yet after all this most of them did not obey God, and he destroyed them in the wilderness.

TO WARN OF THE AWESOMENESS OF DIS-OBEDIENCE AFTER A MIRACLE TO SUPPLY NEEDS OF GOD'S PEOPLE

1 Cor. 12:7, 10: The Holy Spirit displays God's power through each of us as a means of helping the entire church . . . He gives power for doing miracles to some, . . .

TO HELP THE ENTIRE CHURCH

1 Cor 12:28: Here is a list of some of the parts he has placed in his church, which is his body: . . . Those who do miracles, . . .

THOSE WHO DO MIRACLES ARE A PART OF THE BODY OF CHRIST

Heb. 2-4:   For since the messages from angels have always proved true and people have always been punished for disobeying them, what makes us think that we can escape if we are indifferent to this great salvation announced by the Lord Jesus himself, and passed on to us by those who heard him speak? God always has shown us that these messages are true by signs and wonders and various miracles and by giving certain special abilities from the Holy Spirit to those who believe; yes, God has assigned such gifts to each of us.

TO PROVE THAT MESSAGES FROM GOD ARE TRUE

God used miracles in the Old Testament primarily to let the people know that he was their living, ever-present God to supply all their needs and to show his love, mercy and grace for the care and redemption of his children.

Jesus used miracles in the New Testament primarily to prove that he was sent from heaven to save the lost.

When the book of Revelation becomes present tense, Jesus will be bringing everything to pass to wind up the ages and present everything to God as he totally defeats Satan and his powers. Satan, in his last and great effort to win all to himself, does mighty miracles, but no longer do God and Jesus need to prove anything. IT IS FINISHED!

HOW MANY WAYS CAN GOD DO A MIRACLE?

We're always fascinated to discover that you can't put God in a little box, because he always does things differently! Read how God did special miracles in special ways.

GOD CAN EVEN HEAL ... THROUGH A BOOK!

From GARY, INDIANA . . . . . Over the past ten years, my health had steadily regressed. My family spared no expense, and yet one anguishing year followed another. DOZENS of lengthy hospitalizations (sometimes lasting two to three months), four major abdominal exploratory surgeries, several minor ones, endless testing and retesting. After exhausting local physicians, I began seeing specialists in Chicago with repeat visits to the Mayo Clinic.

I underwent psychiatric treatment following a nervous breakdown resulting from the strain on my household and my endurance. While hospitalized for this disorder, I became a "tentative" Christian groping for an understanding of God's plan for me. Had I been wrong in fighting so hard for so long? I couldn't accept the growing invalidism. Why Lord?

After my return from Mayo's in January of this year, I was told I must spend the rest of my life confined to a wheelchair. By this time, I had lost complete use of my right leg and was unable to raise my arms more than half-way. There was extensive swelling and discoloration. It was diagnosed as a progressive muscular deterioration (i.e. M.S.), but I was sent home to await further symptoms for a definite "labelling."

I was instructed to remain in my wheelchair except for three minutes per hour on crutches. Extensive exercises, heat lamps and therapy were begun. The Visiting Nurses Association came daily to assist with the physical therapy. My weight fell to less than 90 pounds — and I'm 5' 8" tall. Because of the intense pain, it became necessary for me to be taught to give myself intra-muscular shots every four hours around the clock. (100 cc. Talwin) The lethargy they provided masked my emotions but during the long, pain-filled nights the questioning went on — why Lord? It became for all just a matter of time. Late one night, I sat alone reading several religious books (God is Fabulous and I Believe in Miracles) given to me by my born-again Christian sister, Barbara. While reading, I felt the need to stop and pray for my husband, Norm — who with my complete helplessness, four children, house and job to manage was nearing the breaking point. As I started soundlessly to pray, a voice distinctly spoke saying, "Lift up your arms to me." I shrugged it off — I hadn't been able to raise my arms in months. It came again, "Lift up your arms to me."

At this point I became irritated as I couldn't concentrate on my prayers for Norm. I started to mentally retort, became exasperated when the voice persisted, and shouted, "See, I can't raise my arms" — and as I spoke, I realized my arms were over my head and I was ON MY FEET MOVING!

In an aura I can only describe as a mystical golden haze, and to the sound of a beautiful choir singing a gospel hymn of my childhood (Softly and Tenderly Jesus is Calling), I felt the presence of Jesus at my right side. His presence was so absolute, I felt no need to face him. I was completely unaware of surroundings, movement or time. I do know we walked, cried and rejoiced together. Human words are just inadequate to describe the experience, but it was so real! Upon "awakening" (as nearly as

I could estimate some 15 minutes later), I knew I had been given a glimpse of heaven. Beautiful beyond compare — an absence of all earthly emotions except an encirclement of complete love — pouring from me to Jesus and back again.

In the ensuing days the swelling and purple discoloration left. My strength and weight increased. In a short time my social worker was able to discontinue the services of a daily homemaker. The Visiting Nurses cut their visits down to bi-weekly, then weekly, and when all skepticism was removed, closed my case. My recovery was complete! PTL! Oh the joy of being needed again rather than needing. For weeks I was unable to share with anyone what had taken place that night. It was such a personal relationship with Jesus. I was afraid that in repeating my story I would lose the true feelings that I found so hard to verbalize. But I have seen so many of those (who knew what I had been going through for so very long) moved to a reaffirmation of their faith, that it became a necessity to share my gift.

Hopefully there will be those reading this who will realize there is but one healer — Jesus Christ. He is alive and with us today wherever we may be. He alone chooses where and when we shall meet — whether it be a lofty cathedral or simple country church. But, I also now know a miracle can come late at night, in an empty room, to a struggling Christian — one who had to be broken mentally and physically before accepting Christ.

Not until I lifted my eyes to Jesus could he lift me. And so, that's my story. Jesus touched me. Mind, body and spirit were made whole.

Praise the Lord — I LIVE!

From INDIANAPOLIS, IND. . . . . . Many thanks for your book WHY SHOULD I SPEAK IN TONGUES? I never thought this was anything that I needed, but after reading your book, the beautiful language came without my even asking for it. Praise the Lord, I have never felt so near him before. My private worship through this experience has greatly expanded and joy has come into my life which is unexplainable.

From TEXAS . . . I've had your book SINCE JESUS PASSED BY laying around for months intending to read it, but failed. I sat down to watch the news and reached for your book. I opened it at random, one of those "Jesus-caused accidents," and it opened to page 42 and I began to read the letter from a girl who had been healed of an allergy. My problem of allergy or sinus is GONE FOREVER. You said Matthew 7:7, and I did, and he did! I instantly felt my head opening up. I can breathe! I just got up and flushed all my medicine away. I don't need it any more.

From NORTH CAROLINA . . . . . I am writing this letter to thank you for your book "GOD IS FABU-LOUS." Two years ago when I was about to the end of my rope a friend gave me a copy of your book. I started reading it one Saturday afternoon and could not put it down. While reading your book at the age of 27, I realized that I had never really met Jesus. After reading the book I dropped to my knees and asked him into my heart and life. Praise the Lord! Jesus came in and changed my whole life. I jumped up from my knees, ran out doors and walked around my yard singing at the top of my lungs "Jesus Saves." Two short months after my exper-ience my husband also accepted Christ and now we have a wonderful Christian home. It all started with GOD IS FABULOUS!

Is the miracle you need a FAT one? Read these!

From CALIFORNIA . . . . . Your book has had a tremendous effect on my life. I weighed in at 336 pounds on my doctor's scale. Since going on the Daniel Fast I have lost 30 pounds in a few weeks' time.

From COLORADO . . . . . Praise God for the Fat book. What a great lesson it teaches us. We think of giving things over to God, but we seem to think our appetites belong to us. I lost the 10 pounds I needed to lose. A friend who could never lose weight lost 10 pounds also. All of this was in three weeks time.

From PENNSYLVANIA . . . . . I lost 83 pounds since I read your book in January.

From ARIZONA . . . . . During a session at one of your meetings you pointed at me and asked, "Wouldn't you like to have a hot fudge sundae?" I was embarrassed, but I realize now that God did the pointing. Praise the Lord. It was just what I needed. Since reading your book I have lost 31 pounds and feel great.

GOD CAN HEAL . . . THROUGH T.V.

From IOWA . . . . . I had been sick with the flu for a week and it really had me down and unable to move. I would be up for fifteen minutes at a time doing my household jobs and then I would have to rest an hour.

I had asked a friend to come for dinner on Sunday, and I was determined to be on my feet for Sunday School and church and to prepare my company meal. But I was no better. I could hardly stand I was so weak. My husband told me to go lie down and he wouldn't let me go to church.

After the family left I turned on TV. When you prayed for healings and miracles I prayed too and the tears ran down my face . . . When you finished I sat there with my eyes closed, waiting for my miracle. Suddenly I realized I could breathe through both nostrils and my sinuses had been plugged solid.

I praised the Lord and jumped up and every symptom and sign of the flu was gone. I ran through the house, jumping up and down for joy and constantly thanking Jesus and praising him for I was healed completely.

From OHIO . . . . . During the prayer with you over the TV, I was touched and healed by Jesus and have not had nor craved a cigarette in over three weeks. Praise God!

From INDIANA . . . . . Several weeks ago Charles prayed for those watching your program and stated that if they had anything wrong with their knees to do as he instructed and he would pray for them. I had had knee trouble for a period of months and it was getting worse

(I'm only 58) so I believed and had faith and I was completely healed and am feeling fine. I thank Charles, but always give credit where credit is due — to the Lord!

From CALIFORNIA . . . . . My husband went to church, but I stayed home because of a severe eye infection. My eye hurt so badly it made me nauseated to even touch it. It was also swollen.

That night, at the end of your program, Charles asked TV viewers to put their hand where they needed healing. Somehow, alone in the living room, I had felt the Holy Spirit move all through your testimonies. I felt God's power unlimited, so I touched my eye as you both prayed.

When I touched my eye it hurt so badly I almost got sick, so I just cupped my hand over the swelling and prayed with you. Suddenly, when you had finished, I touched my eye — it didn't hurt! I felt it gently, no pain! I rubbed it and felt absolutely no pain.

The swelling was gone and it hasn't hurt since!

From BIRMINGHAM, ALABAMA . . . . . I was watching your TV program and you spoke just to me! Four weeks before I had hurt my left knee very badly. It was so severe I was put in the hospital for several days. I was also scheduled to go back to the hospital for possible surgery. I had been in pain all this time, and could hardly walk by dragging my leg. As I watched your TV program this Sunday morning, Charles looked straight at me and said, "Someone is watching this program this morning with a knee problem." Then he said, "If you will lay your hand on the knee and believe God as we pray, God will heal the knee."

I said to myself, "THAT'S ME!"

By the time we had finished praying I could bend my knee without pain. Before, I could not even bend it any. I went to church that morning walking normally. I asked my pastor if I could testify, and told all the people of my healing.

I am the commander of a group of Royal Ranger boys in our church and we planned a four day campout the next week. Included was a hike up a mountain three and a half miles almost straight up.

I am proud to testify to the fact I made this campout, including the hike, without any problem. I have worked ever since. I give God all the praise and glory!.

GOD CAN HEAL — THROUGH THE LAYING ON OF HANDS!

From AUSTRALIA . . . . . For seven years, I was a "battered wife." My first husband was not a drinker, but on occasion he would fly into the most terrible rages and assault me. When the children were born, he turned his rage towards them, too. It was very seldom that at least one of us did not have a bruised and battered body or a cut and bleeding head. I have no idea what made him this way. I did discover that he had attacked other girls before I met him, but I did not know that when we were married. Our son particularly enraged him, and he bears scars on his face in mute testimony to the cruelty of this man. As well as physical beatings, my son was subjected to verbal abuse of the crudest and most vulgar kind. He was told so often he was stupid when his childish hands failed to master a task when he was trying so hard to please. Consequently, from about age two, he began to wet the bed.

After seven years, I decided to leave and took the children with me. I went back to complete my nursing training, and my son began to develop behavioral problems as well. He lied, stole, and generally became anti-social. I was desperate, and after trying psychiatric treatment, placed both the children in a Family Group Home.

The psychiatrist would tell Michael, "You are naughty because you have problems." Michael immediately began to justify his every misdeed with, "I have problems, so I have to be naughty." In the home he didn't improve. Always withdrawn, he suffered because of the bedwetting as the other children would laugh at him.

I moved to Brisbane and, shortly after, I had a seven-hour operation on my spine as a result of injuries received myself. I was in plaster for months. I left for a six weeks' holiday in the States and Canada, and came home much refreshed and able to cope. By this time, I was a Spirit-filled Christian of a few months. The children remained in the Home while I began to work to see if I could continue and support them, with a view to getting them back into my care.

The Lord knew my weaknesses and I met Ian, whom I married. We took the children into our care and moved to the country. Michael improved only slightly and was a source of concern continually to both of us. Mike's bed-wetting continued to be a problem, and he wasn't a little boy now, but a big strapping lad of nearly fourteen.

He enjoyed your first meeting at the Brisbane City Hall. We had driven 110 miles to be there, and we came with an air of expectancy. "Go up and be prayed for, Mike," I suggested as a line of people headed for the stage. Mike went. I watched with excitement and a prayer as he was slain under the power of the Holy Spirit.

I don't even know which of you laid hands on him, but this I do know: Michael is healed of the dreadful bed-wetting, and his personality has undergone a marked change. He is outgoing and honest, has held a part-time job and been found trustworthy, and now aims to become a police officer.

We stand in awe at this great work of God and praise and glorify him. Mike's testimony was, and is, a tremendous demonstration of the power of Jesus!

GOD CAN HEAL — THROUGH A PRAYER CLOTH!

From FAILSWORTH, ENGLAND . . . . . Thank you for your prayers and the prayer cloth for our baby. I put the cloth in his little hand and we prayed for his head to be healed. I know you won't be surprised when you hear the reaction of the two doctors who saw him. They said, "This baby never had a dislocated hip, and there is NOTHING wrong with his head." He was born with a waterhead and a dislocated hip, but was healed completely by the little prayer cloth. Praise God the anointing of God stayed during the flight across the ocean

From LOUISIANA . . . . . I put the prayer cloth in my husband's pillow case and within 2 weeks he was saved. He sure was miserable from the moment I put it there as God dealt with him. Thank you, Jesus!

GOD CAN HEAL — WHILE YOU'RE RIDING IN A CAR

"On the way home from your service, my big toe which has bothered me for years, was healed."

"I was so disappointed when I left your service because I hadn't been healed, but when we were about 60 miles from the meeting the power of God went through my body and I was instantly healed. I had come on a stretcher and left on a stretcher, but walked out of the station wagon whole when we got home!"

"I was still hurting when I left your meeting, but in the car on the way home, my bursitis was completely healed and the pain left! This was a year ago and it has never returned. Praise God!"

GOD CAN HEAL — BY PROXY

From TEXAS . . . . . Do you remember that little Episcopal church where we prayed for a girl with cancer who was not expected to live through the day? You looked at your watch and said, "It's 11:37." You'll never believe this, but a friend of mine went to the hospital to visit Shirley, and when she got there she was dancing in the Spirit in her room. She said, "Shirley, what happened to you?" Shirley replied, "At 11:37 this morning, Jesus Christ walked into this room and said, 'You're healed, get out of bed.' I knew he was real, so I pulled the needle out of my arm and walked out of my room into the hall to tell the nurses that Jesus had visited me. They were really shocked!" Shirley was discharged from the hospital completely healed two days later.

GOD CAN HEAL — DURING WORSHIP

In Racine, Wisconsin we saw one of the most unusual miracles we've ever seen. While we were worshipping God, a young girl sitting in the audience said, "Mother, my teeth are moving in my mouth." The mother said, "Get up there real quick to where they are." As a friend of ours was screening the people coming forward, she looked at the little girl's teeth, and saw tartar, raw gums which looked like they had been "over-flossed" and crooked teeth. The girl had been to the orthodontist the month before, but because of being one of nine children her parents could not afford the work. The girl went under the power and 30 minutes later when she came out she had the most beautiful, perfect, straight white teeth we've ever seen. They looked like they had been created out of heavenly pearls and put right in her mouth. There was a dentist there who had driven four and a half hours to be at the meeting. We called him to the stage and he, like all of us, was completely awe-stricken at what God had done. Thank you, Jesus!

God inhabits the praises of his people! Let's praise him more!

GOD CAN HEAL — AND LET YOU KNOW LATER!

From CORPUS CHRISTI, TEXAS . . . . . . I have suffered with hayfever all my life. During hayfever season I was sneezing, dripping, wheezing and miserable. You prayed and I thought the hayfever season had ended, and didn't realize I was healed until the next year when it never came back.

Frances Hunter: I lost a filling from one of my teeth while we were in Florida, and threw it in the waste basket in a church. When I got home I made an appointment with the dentist, and as I drove up to his office I said, "God, you healed five people the other night by filling their teeth. How come you didn't fill mine?" When the dental technician and the dentist examined my tooth, they couldn't find the hole where the filling was missing . . . and neither could I!

GOD CAN HEAL — DURING WORD OF KNOWLEDGE

A man sat in the balcony talking to himself. "This is phony. Nobody's being healed. They're just imagining the things they're calling out as being healed. How can you tell what's going on. I can't see anything happening. How do I know they're healed?"

"Someone in the balcony is being healed of a lump under his arm." Charles had a word of knowledge and called it out like all the other ones, but it went straight to the heart of the man who had been talking to himself, because he was the one who had come with a tumor under his arm about the size of a softball. It was very painful and he was miserable. The finger pointed right at him.

What was happening? The pain disappeared, and his arm went to his side naturally. He felt under his arm and couldn't find anything. He felt inside his coat, and couldn't find anything! The tumor was gone!

He raced down to the stage and said he had been "hounded" by friends to come to this meeting. He claimed to be an agnostic, but when he realized the power of God was real, he said, "I'm not an agnostic any more!"

> Jesus' disciples saw him do many other miracles besides the ones told about in this book, but these are recorded so that you will believe that he is the Messiah, the Son of God, and that believing in him you will have life. (John 20:30-31)

GOD CAN HEAL — ANY WAY HE WANTS TO!

A VISION IS A MIRACLE!

by Frances

FIVE YEARS AGO, I WOULDN'T HAVE BELIEVED THIS, BUT NOW I DO!

The final night of a Delightfully Charismatic Christian Walk Seminar in Calgary, Canada, was a night of power like we've never seen in our entire ministry.

Faith was at top level because of the seminar teachings. That night's subject was marriage, and as Charles was talking about honesty in marriage, I felt such a tremendous wave of power I nearly fell over. I grabbed the podium and looked over at Charles to see if he felt the same thing I did.

I couldn't believe my eyes!

Out of the ends of his fingers were shooting flames of blue fire about four inches long, and as I looked at them, God spoke to me and said, "The healing anointing is upon Charles. The first thirty people who reach the altar will be instantly healed!"

I had to interrupt Charles! The power was increasing to such an extent I knew God had something special! I repeated to the audience what God had said, and it looked like the entire auditorium turned upside-down. I never saw sick and crippled people move so fast in my entire life!

As Charles ran off the stage to lay hands on them, the power of God was so strong they fell in waves as he ran

through the crowd. When he was about half-way across
the front of the auditorium, he raised his hands to touch
some, and about thirty to forty people fell under the
power at the same time. People began weeping all over
the auditorium as they felt the power of God in a way
they had never felt it before.

Bob and Joan were offstage at this particular moment,
but they felt something supernatural come through even
the loudspeaker. Bob said, "I heard Frances say, 'Get out
of the way and let Charles through,' then I heard the
word 'fire!' I came running out as fast as I could, wondering if there had been a bomb of some kind or other.
There was — A HOLY GHOST BOMB! Charles was plow-
ing through the crowd and people were falling all over the
place!"

Joan said, "I kept hearing 'let him through, let him
through, there's fire on his hands,' so I ran to the curtain
at the back of the stage. The power of God was so strong
it felt exactly like a solid wall of God's beautiful power,
and I broke into tears, completely overcome by the overwhelming presence of God."

By this time Charles had gone almost across the auditorium, and the flames began to diminish, and finally
they disappeared. He came back up onto the stage, and
asked the people to raise their hands if they KNEW they
were healed. More than 100 hands were raised, as God
gave even more than he had promised.

It is impossible to explain how you feel in a moment
like this. I was so awed by what I had seen and heard that
I just stood there wondering what was going to happen
next!

I didn't have to wait but just a few seconds and then I
saw things I had never seen in my entire life. The Jubilee
Auditorium is a large auditorium with two balconies, and
an extremely high ceiling. As I looked out over the people, there appeared a huge dove with a wingspread of
about fifty feet hovering on the left-hand side of the
auditorium.

It was not white!

Instead, it was "like as of fire."

The dove looked exactly as if it had been carved right out of fire! It was red, orange and yellow!

I have never felt the awesome presence of God as I did at that moment, then a shocking thing began to happen!

The quills from the wings of the dove began flying out across the audience and landing on various people.

It looked like skyrockets exploding as the quills flew faster and faster across the auditorium.

God spoke again and said, "There is perversion in the sexual life of married couples here. There is adultery in marriages here, and I am sending the fire of my Holy Spirit to burn it out."

Men and women began weeping as they cried out, "God save me!"

The presence of God was a reality to many people who had never before felt his presence.

The convicting power of the Holy Spirit was upon many marriages . . . then,

As suddenly as it had appeared, the dove disappeared!

It was instantly replaced by a white dove.

I told the audience the dove "like as of fire" had disappeared and had been replaced by a white one, and waited for another message from God because I didn't understand this at all.

God gave Charles the message this time and he said, "I have sent my white dove as a symbol of purification. Your marriages have been cleansed and purified. Keep them that way!"

The white dove was gone!

Hundreds of people accepted Jesus as a result of this awe-inspiring moment and many were baptized in the Holy Spirit and healed at the same time. It was estimated that around 1,800 people fell under the power of God this one night.

We may never again stand in the Shekinah glory of God until we get to heaven, but our lives will never be the same again as a result of this night.

Some people might not believe it; maybe you won't, but we have to, because we were there!

An IMPOSSIBLE MIRACLE, but it happened!

DO YOU WANT A MIRACLE?

TODAY is your miracle day! Let's believe God for whatever you need, because there's an "impossible miracle" waiting for you.

Our mail is full of interesting letters; some sad, some heartbreaking, but many joyous ones telling us of "impossible miracles" that have happened. There was a time when we thought the only miracle worth sharing was one where someone walked out of a wheelchair, but how many people need this kind of a miracle?

We have discovered the important miracle is the one YOU need! And any miracle is a BIG miracle when it happens to you.

A back healing might not seem to be a BIG miracle to you, unless it happened to be YOUR back that was hurting!

A "crick" in the neck might seem insignificant to you, unless the "crick" was in YOUR neck!

A headache seems like a minor thing, unless the head that's aching is YOUR own!

A sore elbow is nothing, is it? That is, unless the elbow that's sore is YOURS!

Cigarette smoking is something you just use your own will power to stop. Unless YOU happen to be the one who's addicted! Then it takes a miracle of God to deliver you!

A stiff knee might seem unimportant to you, unless YOU were the one hobbling along on it!

Many of the letters that reach our office contain "little" miracles, and yet as we read them one after another, our faith really ignites when we realize that God cares for the "little" problems in our life. Maybe your miracle, large or small, will match one that we're sharing. Trust God for it as you read.

These miracles have come from almost every state in the Union and cover almost every kind of a miracle you could need. You will notice many of these people did not know they were healed until a later time. You will also notice many came to services NOT EXPECTING TO BE HEALED! You may not believe right now and yet God wants to do a supernatural, wonderful thing in your life!

From NEW YORK . . . . . When you were at Buffalo you prayed over me for the healing of my elbows. I have had psoriasis on both elbows all my life. I am 42. Everything was done, bought, tried for them to NO AVAIL. Last summer I had even asked my doctor to put me in the hospital and scrape, sand, operate, graft or do SOMETHING for them. He said I would have to just "learn to live with it." Praise the Lord, as I was leaving the service that night, Jesus said to my spirit, "Go and be prayed for your elbows. I (Jesus) cleansed the lepers and I can and will make your elbows just as clean." You know already what I'm going to write!!!!! Praise and thank you, dear Jesus, three days later my elbows were COMPLETELY HEALED!

From WISCONSIN . . ... At your meeting in Green Bay last April a friend of mine was healed and has never worn her back brace since. Praise the Lord!

From MICHIGAN . . . . . In July of 1974 my husband received healing for his back after suffering for 18 years. I came to that meeting at FA-HO-LO Park, Grass Lake, Michigan on crutches which I have not used since nor do I even need my cane any more!! Hallelujah!

From IOWA . . . . .A bus load of us and our past minister went to see you in Cedar Falls, Iowa. To be honest I didn't believe a thing that was done at the morning miracle service. I really thought you were a phony and I was ready to come home. But Praise the Lord, the evening service CHANGED MY LIFE! I was healed of backaches which I have had for years. I have doctored and had treatments for years because of a curve in my spine. Thank God for all of you who could bring a soul like me to Christ.

From INDIANA . . . . . I did not know it at the time, but I received a healing from a spastic colon. Frances called me from the audience and said God had a special touch for me, and I was slain in the Spirit for the first time. Now I am healed! I have not taken medicine in about 3 weeks, and before, I could not go one whole day without medicine. Three months later I went to the doctor. He said when he originally diagnosed it that I would probably have this condition for the rest of my life if I did not stay on medication. When I went back to him, he did not use the word "cured." He said, "These things happen sometimes." P.T.L. I KNOW THEY DO — after prayer!

From LaCROSSE, WISCONSIN . . . . . It was towards the end of the service when we were worshipping the Lord that the Spirit of the Lord fell on the auditorium and many fell under the power of God. That happened to me! Hallelujah! Charles gave instructions that we were to lay hands on the parts of our body where we needed healing, so I laid my hands on my eyes and fell under the power. THE LORD TOLD ME that my eyes were healed! I didn't believe him until the following Monday when the Lord confirmed his word. THE DOCTOR TOLD ME I no longer needed to wear glasses. I give God all the glory!

From NEBRASKA . . . . . I went forward at the meeting in Ottumwa to be delivered of tranquilizers as a crutch. I asked that God help me lean upon him instead of pills when fear and worry overtook me — especially fear of sickness — cancer. I fell under the power and have not taken a tranquilizer since.

From MICHIGAN . . . . . In November of 1973, I had to have a laminectomy, which was surgery on a deteriorated disc. My spine had to be scraped due to arthritis and bones had to be put in place. After surgery I had to have therapy on my right leg because of the spine problem. It was very difficult to raise my right leg and I had to take my hand and raise it to cross my legs. Whenever I got into a car I had to lift my leg in order to get myself into the car. At night it was difficult for me to roll over in bed or to get up or down without crying out from the terrific pain.

Praise the Lord! He is my healer! He reached down and touched me with his healing power as we were praising him. My right leg became numb and I was impressed to start exercising my legs and back. I was healed! Praise the Lord! He touched me!

Frances asked me to come to the platform and tell what the Lord had done for me and she prayed and I was slain in the Spirit. As I returned to my seat, I realized I was able to lift my leg and cross it over my left leg without any help. As the service was being dismissed we all stood and the Lord impressed me to put my legs together and for the first time in my life MY LEGS WERE NOT BOWED, they were completely straight! The next day I asked my father to look at my legs and he said, "What happened to your legs? Did someone break them and straighten them?" I replied, "The LORD healed them!" Hallelujah!

From MINNESOTA . . . . . My son was receiving two serum shots each week at the age of 18 months. My husband is a distance runner, and our boys wanted to run like their dad. At age 12, Bob couldn't run a mile. He came home with chest pains and was wheezing. Sunday evening as you were sharing, Bob had chest pains again and when you called for children, he asked if he could go forward. I told him to ask his dad and they went forward together. My husband hasn't fully understood my newness in Christ, and I'm sure many times I've left him scratching his head wondering what had happened to his wife. My prayer was that he would take us that night and see the power for himself!

As Frances prayed, my son said he felt a tightness in his chest (like someone was squeezing him) and then he felt a tingling all over and went under the power. He later went forward to receive the baptism with the Holy Sprit.

On Monday, Bob went running with his dad. I knew this was it and decided not to pray ASKING, but to pray THANKING! Later Bob came in the house, his eyes and mouth pale from running. All he could say was, "I did it, I did it, I did it!" I asked him if his chest hurt or if he was wheezing. Bob said, "No, but my legs are killing me." PRAISE THE LORD. The next night he even ran two miles.

He has had people say it is impossible, God doesn't heal, he can't do anything. Bob knows better! Of our four children I felt it would be hardest for Bob to find Christ. He is well-liked, has many friends and really doesn't need anything. God in his beauty and perfection knew just what Bob needed and just how to reach him. Bob's eyes now twinkle for the Lord, because he touched him in a grand way. Last week in rough, choppy waters, he swam the MILE swim and received the Mile Swim Award. Bob said he would never have tried it before. We give all the glory to God!

From IOWA . . . . . Our daughter is 8½ years of age. She had ear surgery in July of 1973. She had so much infection in her left ear that they had to take a lot of the bone out and also part of the ear drum. There wasn't even enough left for them to do much with. She was in surgery nine hours and she was deaf in her left ear. She went forward when you called for anyone with hearing problems, and came back hearing!

We took her to her doctor and he gave her a hearing test. His bottom jaw about touched the floor and the papers shook in his hands. He looked at us and asked where we had been taking her. Christine asked us if she could tell him and we told her to tell him anything she wanted to. He could tell she was full of joy. She told him that Jesus had healed her ear. Her doctor looked at her for a second and then said, "Well, that's good enough for me, because I didn't do it!"

From FLORIDA . . . . . I had Paget's disease, a bone disease, for at least fifteen years. Very seldom was I without pain in my back, arms or legs. I fell at work in 1968 fracturing a vertebra in the diseased lower back. I was unable to work after that. The pain made it impossible for me to sit still for even a short time.

On March 6, 1975 at The Assembly of God Church in Lakeland, Florida at the Hunters' service in the evening I went forward praying for a healing. I had always been a Methodist. My back was hurting so bad, I had contemplated getting up and going out to exercise a bit. I told Mrs. Hunter this, she prayed for me and as she ran her hand down my back, the pain all left and I have had no pain to this day.

God also healed my right bad shoulder. I had been unable to raise my arm straight up for years, or to use it normally, but it is perfect now. I have been in hospitals several times for asthma, but since that miracle service I have had no trouble at all. A few days later I realized I had also been cured of hemorrhoids which I had for years. GOD HAS SURELY HEALED ME!

From INDIANA . . . . . I thank the Lord every day for he touched me with his healing power when you prayed for me. I said "hiatal hernia." You put your finger on my stomach and prayed a short prayer. I was slain in the Spirit. While lying on the floor I could feel the healing power working on the inside of my body. I came home and ate a good dinner, went to bed early and slept all night without waking up until morning. I had my bed raised 7 inches at the head. Now I have taken the blocks out and can lie flat without any more heartburn, and no trouble with food coming up in my mouth if I stoop over after eating. Praise the Lord!

From KANSAS..... When you came to Wichita I only had 25¢ to put in the offering, but you asked God to multiply it 100 fold. Not long after that I was asked to give a talk about fostering two college classes and was given $25. It was such a shock to be paid for talking, it took me months to cash the check and finally realized that God had multiplied my gift 100 fold. Thank you, Jesus!

From COLUMBUS, OHIO..... When I was five and a half months pregnant with my first child, I was in an automobile accident and was thrown out of the car and received a hard blow on the head. This caused severe headaches and blacking out, and I discovered I had epilepsy. When I came up for prayer at that meeting, I was slain in the Spirit, and while under the power I felt like God gently sawed off the top of my head, brushed out the cobwebs, and then gently put the top of my head back on. Up until that time I had terrible, nauseating, exhausting headaches, and that is all gone now. I have not had any medication since then and it is over two years. Praise God!

From NEBRASKA..... Things really happened when we went to your meeting! My husband had been warned of the dangers of the Charismatic movement for about thirty minutes before going to your meeting, but he went forward to receive the baptism in the Holy Spirit. On Friday night my arm was lengthened by the Lord almost one inch. I had always had trouble with pain between my shoulder blades when working in the kitchen or typing, and now it is completely gone! P.T.L. My husband was cured of cigarette smoking. Two of our children went forward to receive the baptism! Glory! What a night with the Lord!

Saturday morning my husband went to your teaching session and came home with almost every book you had ever written and bubbling over, as much as a reserved and quiet man bubbles!

Saturday night the presence of the Lord was so real as you said a healing cloud was over us. Our Sunday School teacher was healed of hypoglycemia during that service! We had been praying for her for months.

This same night you prayed for anointing of husbands' and wives' hands and for healing of marriages. We laid hands on each other and several things happened: the lump on my husband's shoulder decreased considerably — a benign lump he had had for over ten years, and a pain at the base of my spine disappeared. Also, when marriages were prayed for, all resentment and bitterness was removed from our marriage — the Holy Spirit swept over us like a gentle breeze and left Bruce crying holy tears and me plopping down in my seat crying!

From WASHINGTON, D.C. . . . . . I have suffered from migraine headaches for 15 years. On February 17, 1974, in the Washington Hilton Hotel, Washington, D.C. at a Full Gospel Business Men's Convention I was slain in the Spirit when Charles prayed for me. I did not remember him touching me, but while under the power I felt waves of love passing through my body. It seems as though I lay there quite a long time, and I remember I did not want to get up·because the feeling was so peaceful and there was LOVE all around me, and complete assurance from God that he was going to take care of me and my family. As I returned to my seat I was aware that I had been healed, and I have not had a headache since. Praise the Lord!

From NEBRASKA . . . . . Last summer I had a job at an inside pool for the YMCA. I had classes for about 75 kids at the same time. I had to yell constantly every day for about eight hours, not out of anger, but because that's the only way to be heard. For nearly a year and a half since then I've been having trouble with my throat, and since I am a singer this was difficult. During this time I lost over an octave in my voice range so I could only sing songs with a range of about eight notes. Some days I could barely whisper. I kept telling myself that it would go away, but it persisted. It got worse and worse, until some mornings I couldn't talk at all.

Finally, in July of 1974, I went to see a well-known throat specialist in town. He told me I had a very severe case of nodules on my vocal chords and put me on six months' vocal rest. That meant NO singing, yelling, loud laughing, and as little talking as possible. He said if the problem persisted for an additional three months I would have to have surgery to have them removed.

Needless to say, I was very upset. I quit my job and had several weeks of bewilderment, and then in August my husband and I went to a Hunter meeting in Omaha, not with my healing in mind at all, but to learn. The thought of being healed crept into my mind, and I was really excited. Someone was healed of cancer and I thought, "That's great, but they'll probably never get around to little diseases like mine!!"

Then they had the married couples stand and they prayed that God would anoint their hands. When my husband laid hands on my throat, I KNEW I HAD BEEN HEALED! I cried and cried, and the Lord really cleaned me out on the inside.

The following Monday, only two days later, I had an appointment with the throat specialist to get checked. I sat in the waiting room for an hour reading Psalms in anticipation of what I would soon hear. When the doctor looked at my throat, he said, "I can see where the nodules have been, but they're gone. I really don't understand it. It's IMPOSSIBLE!" He rechecked a couple of times and said, "They're gone — you can lead a normal speaking and singing life."

Praise the Lord! I have been singing and talking ever since with not one speck of trouble. I have not had a hoarse note since. All the glory goes to God and I praise him for his love and power and how he manifested it on me. I am a Methodist!

From ARKANSAS . . . . . I have had osteoporosis of the neck and spine and have spent two years in bed. I have been hospitalized many times for several weeks at a time. I was instantly healed in Ft. Smith, Arkansas, and received the baptism with the Holy Spirit.

From CEDAR RAPIDS, IOWA . . . . . My right nostril had been clogged for a long time. This seems like such a

little thing, but it can be an annoying thing. Consequently, I had trouble breathing, and was always tired
because of lack of air. Finally an eye, ear and nose specialist operated and made a new entrance for my nose. He
said, "You will have difficulty with it, even after the
operation." He was correct! Each morning I would have
to take breathing exercises, BUT NOT ANY LONGER. I
was healed at Sioux City, Iowa, August, 1974, at a
Miracle Service! Praise the Lord!

From VIRGINIA . . . . . For two years, 25 doctors
tried to diagnose my problem, and when an outstanding
endocrinologist finally took my case, he diagnosed it as
Addison's disease. For sixteen years he treated me. When
I went to the meeting in Washington, D.C. you singled me
out as being healed of a kidney infection. I planned to
keep my seat until a jolt of electricity knocked me to my
feet.

Instead of praising the Lord about the kidney infec
tion, I told you of my Addison's disease which doctors
said is incurable. You replied that I had been healed of it.
My mouth flew open and I said, "Really?" You prayed in
tongues squeezing the daylights outa me, then I was slain
in the Spirit. The respiratory specialist had given me
tests of blood, etc. to determine the state of adrenal in-
sufficiency, but after being slain in the Spirit, he gave me
his report, "BEYOND A SHADOW OF A DOUBT
THERE IS NO ADDISON'S DISEASE — YOU ARE
HEALED!"

From TEXAS . . . . . While driving you folk to
Amarillo, Charles was telling of the young girl who had
been healed of a knot on her forehead. At the time that
he was relating this, a lump or knot on my own body
disappeared . . PRAISE GOD!

From MIAMI, FLA. . . . . . For about a year I had felt
something bothering me in my right armpit, but I
couldn't find anything. Then one day I felt a lump there,
so after two months I went to the doctor. He said it was

a swollen gland, but it still didn't go away. When I attended your meeting, the lump was larger than before, and hurt somewhat. When you were praying for healings, it disappeared, and I haven't found it since.

From NEW JERSEY . . . . . For over a year I'd suffered with severe rectal bleeding and a rectocele, facing surgery, because nothing seemed to help. I was slain in the Spirit at your meeting in Allendale, in August last year, and felt an absolute peace and assurance that all was well. Two weeks later the pain and bleeding stopped, I dispensed with my array of medication and have had no problems since! My gynecologist examined me in March and said, "No operation necessary." Praise the Lord!

From HICKORY, N.C. . . . . . When Frances and Charles walked down the aisles at the end of the meeting and touched each person, I asked that God would "store up" enough of his power to touch my mother who had not been able to come. I'm a Southern Baptist!

I went on to Georgia. A week later I returned and prayed with my mother. She was slain in the Spirit. We prayed for the lumps that had been discovered a few weeks before by her doctor, and when she was slain a "volt of current" went through both of us. That night in bed she was praising the Lord in the Spirit and she felt little shocks in her right breast and several "pulling out" sensations. A week later a visit to her doctor confirmed that THE LUMPS WERE GONE! All glory goes to Jesus Christ, the healer of bodies and souls!

From EUGENE, OREGON . . . . . I shall never forget the evening that I first confronted Charles and Frances. It will remain with me until I meet God who worked through these blessed people. I was a very skeptical Christian and I might as well have not been a Christian at all for I had nothing to prove my faith to my fellowman. I had no witness, for the power of God wasn't in my words when I shared with the world about God. Then I saw, with my very own eyes, miraculous works done through Charles and Frances. I was miraculously healed of disbelief in the power of God!

From VIRGINIA BEACH, VA. . . . . . In 1968, the doctors at Ft. Belvoir, Virginia, discovered I had degenerative disease in the bones of both ears called otosclerosis and was on my way to a complete loss of hearing. My hearing became poor enough that the doctor said I needed to have an operation in my right ear. I did and it was successful enough to allow me to continue teaching.

Then in 1973, my hearing was fading rapidly and I knew I could never teach another year. I was distraught over this, but something else began to happen in my life. I began learning about the true love of Jesus. I gave my heart to Jesus and discovered that he is the same yesterday, today, and forever!

I had read your books, and the Lord quickened my heart to be with you in Hickory, North Carolina. This was my first experience at a gathering like this and I have never witnessed healing in other people or witnessed or felt the power of God so greatly. I also had not asked for or received the baptism in the Holy Spirit, and being a Methodist had never been more demonstrative in worship than kneeling. I went to Hickory as an amateur . . . and when it was over, Praise God, I had definitely decided I wanted to be a pro.

Frances, I came up to you before the luncheon and told you I was losing my hearing and had come expecting a miracle. You looked me squarely in the eye when you said P.T.L. and told me that the Lord had revealed to you that morning that he would heal the deaf . . . and HE DID! Thank you, Jesus, I not only received a miraculous healing in my ears, but I also received a glorious baptism in the Holy Spirit and did not come back to Virginia Beach the same person I was when I left.

From ILLINOIS . . . . . I've been a Southern Baptist all my life, and I had been under conviction for almost a year about smoking. I hated myself every time I picked up a cigarette. I tried so hard to quit and it was even worse when un-Christian people I knew quit and I couldn't.

At the meeting I went forward when you asked for people who wanted deliverance from cigarettes and I fell under the power. I only lay there a couple of minutes and when I got up I started crying. I knew something precious had happened.

I've been tempted to take a cigarette, but now the Lord is my will power, praise his name!

From ROBINSON, ILLINOIS . . . . I know that God is working and I shall always cherish our meeting in Springfield and again in Robinson. The desire for tobacco is gone and my daily walk with Jesus grows sweeter each day.

From HOUSTON, TX. . . . . . Frances prayed with me for my ex-husband. She prayed, "Lord, bring him back to his children and his wife and make him a good husband and father." February 2, 1974, we were remarried. We had been separated and divorced for two years. Before this answer to prayer there was no hope for the marriage.

From HOUSTON, TX. . . . . . I had a gold crown on my tooth, and from the moment it was put in, I had severe pain off and on for nearly two weeks.

My dentist told me on the morning of the Hunter meeting that if the pain continued it would be necessary to have an endodontist do a root canal. I was praying for my mother-in-law when Mr. Hunter said someone has been healed of a tooth problem. MY TOOTH WAS IN-STANTLY HEALED BY GOD and I've never had a pain again!

From WISCONSIN . . . . . Having sent you a donation last month, we received a letter from you, in which you asked the Lord to bless us with a hundred times our donation. In that same mail we received an unexpected check for $2,282.98 for crop failure. We were only expecting a couple of hundred dollars, but the Lord had already answered your prayers — Praise God!!!! We had sent in $20.00.

From MICHIGAN . . . . . ALL PRAISE TO GOD! The very day that you would have received our last check, my husband was notified that he had been approved for a $2,000 raise. Also that same day we sold our house in Grand Rapids. The Lord is getting us out of debt!

From DALLAS, TX. . . . . . In Oct. of 1973 I went to your retreat in Waco, Texas. I hadn't been to church in over 20 years. I was 47 at that time, and you asked if anyone wanted to be delivered from smoking. I just laughed, but someone (the Lord) marched me right up on that stage with my cigarettes and a $25.00 lighter, which was collected. You prayed for us, and from that moment on I HAVE NOT TOUCHED A CIGARETTE OR HAD A DESIRE.

From LOUISIANA . . . . . I was in New Orleans at the Theater of Performing Arts at one of your meetings and was delivered from smoking. I had smoked for 57 years and have had no desire for a cigarette since. Thank God!

From INDIANA . . . . . I want to thank God for the way he has used you in my family. My husband received the baptism of the Holy Spirit through your book, THE TWO SIDES OF A COIN, and my father received at your 4th of July meeting in Jackson, Michigan. Although I am a Wesleyan Methodist now, I was raised a Nazarene. My father's Nazarene pastor wrote to you last spring about the baptism of the Holy Spirit. He received and he was the one who brought Dad and Mom to Camp Fa-Ho-Lo in July. On the way to the meeting, Dad was discussing his fanatical daughter who had gone off the deep end spiritually, even speaking in tongues. Jokingly, Dad turned to his Nazarene pastor and said, "Well, I haven't spoken in tongues yet, have you?" Dad literally became ill when his pastor said, "Yes, I have."

Do you remember an older couple who came to you while Charles was praying for the people on the busses before the July 4th service? That was my poor "sick" father who was so afraid of "tongues" that the news of his pastor's defection gave him the tremors. Somehow Dad managed to sit through the evening service, and the Holy Spirit convinced this frightened Christian that "tongues" were of God. The baptism of the Holy Spirit (which Dad received that night) revolutionized his Christian experience. He fell in love with his Bible again, he spends more time in prayer, he won some young people to Christ, and he is filled with joy. That's the real impossible miracle in his case! My father was a joyless Christian that had been bound by worry and fear for as long as I can remember. What a change! Praise the Lord! A month ago Dad called to see if Jim and I wanted to come home for the weekend to have a prayer meeting. Imagine that — for a prayer meeting! Needless to say, we drove the 150 miles and had a glorious time.

From CALIFORNIA . . . . . Jesus had been my Lord ten months and I had prayed for a month to stop smoking. When you came to Calvary Community Church in San Jose, it was a night I'll never forget. My daughter and I were delivered from smoking. I had smoked for 34 years and my daughter had smoked for eleven. This was over four years ago. We haven't smoked, or wanted to from that night on. Praise the Lord!

From TEXAS . . . . . At the meeting at Christ for the Nations in Dallas last year Charles said, "If you give, it will return to you." I had a $5.00 bill and a little change to last me until payday. I said, "Lord, I don't have any money, this that I have goes to pay a bill." My next thought was, "The shape I'm in, what's $5.00?" I put it in the collection plate and forgot about it. When I got paid a few days later I held the envelope in my hands before opening it, prayed, and it had a $50.00 raise. Praise the Lord!

From TEXAS . . . . . I was at one of your meetings at Faith Temple last time you were here. You both prayed for a mass in my right kidney. X-rays show it is gone. Praise the Lord!

From OREGON . . . . . "I've had dyslexia since I was six years old, and I haven't been able to spell right or read right. The b's were all jumbled together and so were the m's and the w's. I couldn't see them. If it was a "b" I thought it was a "d." Then when I wrote them down I always got my "d's" and "b's" mixed up. One time I wrote a sign on my door when I was about eight which said, "CLOSE THIS BOOR — NO DOYS ALLOWED." . . . . My Mom said she would go with me to the Hunter meeting. She felt I should be prayed for. I went up to Charles and asked him to pray for me. He just put his fingers on my eyes and prayed something about rewiring my eyes. I fell back under the power of God. I couldn't believe what was happening. IT WAS FAR OUT! My eyes are terrific today. I got an "A" on a spelling test. My teacher said, "You got all your d's and b's straight to-day." Everything is terrific . . . .

From MICHIGAN . . . . . During your meeting the Lord healed me of a lump in the breast which was first noticed by a doctor in 1968. He also removed a lump from under my arms. This supernatural surgery amazed me, because I had asked for prayer for a skin condition in my face and never even thought about the lumps. Praise the Lord even though I failed to call it to God's atten-tion, he healed me!

From IOWA . . . . . When I came up to be prayed for, I didn't expect God to heal my bursitis, but he did anyway! Hallelujah!

From OREGON . . . . . What a wonderful feeling to go to my doctor for a thyroid test and discover it was per-fectly normal! I have had this problem my entire life!

From CALIFORNIA . . . . . MY HEALING TOOK PLACE BEFORE THE MEETING STARTED! I spoke to you folks while you were autographing books, and as I took a step from the aisle to a seat, the Lord said to me, "YOU HAVE BEEN HEALED." I shifted my weight back and forth and not a pain to be found. (I had been suffering from a lower back problem for over 10 years, the last two in continual pain from the pinched nerve.) I had an extremely awkward walk due to the pain and the fact that all my life one hip was much higher than the other. I did not realize until I got home that evening that not only was my back healed, but also my hips were perfectly aligned. PRAISE THE LORD!

From NEW JERSEY . . . . . HOLY LAUGHTER . . . I laughed and laughed and didn't even know what I was laughing about! But what happened before was not a laughing matter.

It all started at the birth of our baby in July, 1975. The doctors aren't sure yet what the problem was. All they know, and I know is that it has caused me a lot of pain in my back for a long time.

It kept getting worse until I had to go to the hospital for two weeks in February, 1976, and was put in traction. That was not a cure. I continued having difficulty and at times it was so bad I could hardly lift my leg or walk without going into spasms. I took medication for muscle relaxation. At times I had to take extremely heavy medication to even function. At times I could not even put weight on my leg, and sometimes for hours there was no feeling in it. We knew the problem was serious, and hoped that a suggested operation would not be necessary. One hip was about a half inch lower than the other and one arm was shorter than the other.

On August 22, 1976, Gary and I went to a Charismatic meeting conducted by Charles and Frances Hunter.

The service had hardly started when Frances stepped to the microphone and said God had just told her that there were a lot of people there who were not saved, or were in doubt as to whether they had been born again. She asked them to come upon the large stage of the auditorium. We were amazed as about two or three hundred people moved quickly forward. They hadn't even preached or done anything! It was the Holy Spirit moving supernaturally to prepare the people's souls before he was ready to prepare their bodies for healing in the miracle service which was to follow. This seemed to electrify the faith of the audience.

After this they asked God for a mass healing of backs. We all measured our arms and it was amazing to see about two hundred people remain standing with uneven-length arms!

What they didn't know that I knew was that one of my arms was shorter than the other. I didn't want anyone to know this or see it, so I put my hands in back of me. I thought nobody saw me, but God did and he said, "Hey, I want to bless you, but how can I unless you cooperate?" It didn't take me but a second to respond to him, and out went my arms in front of me.

One of the ushers saw my short arm and selected me to go to the stage. I briefly explained about the back problem and pain that had existed since our child was born.

Suddenly the arm began growing out and I fell over backwards!

It was beautiful as a wave of God swept over me.

As I lay there, I began laughing and laughing and couldn't stop!

I didn't even know what I was laughing about, but neither did I care.

God was blessing me beyond anything I had expected.

When I got up, I discovered THERE WAS NO PAIN! It was gone! We checked my hips and God had evened them up.

What happened next really shocked me even more!

For some time I had been having a tough time walking like Jesus wanted me to. I had previously been in the occult but had been delivered from that. It seemed I would turn left and then right, away from the path God was telling me he wanted me to walk. Charles looked intently at me and said, "Walk in the straight and narrow way!" I knew it wasn't Charles saying that, but the Spirit of God telling me to walk where he wanted me to walk, and not go where I had been going!

Since the moment I was touched by the power of the Holy Spirit on that stage as my arm grew out and my hips were leveled, I have had absolutely no pain and no problems. It was an instant, complete miracle of God!

Perhaps even more important was the way he has blessed our life and marriage. We have been reading the Bible more, and I have been much easier for Gary to live with, too! I have made a much deeper consecration to the Lord and am determined to live for him. Jesus did miracles while he was on earth so that people would believe, and it certainly made a more realistic believer out of me when Jesus touched me and healed me, inside and out!

NOW IT'S YOUR TURN . . . One of the most exciting times in your life is when YOU need a miracle!

A woman came to a meeting in Oregon needing a unique miracle because she had never been able to get her knees closer together than three inches because of an accident. She was healed instantly by the power of God and her legs and body straightened out. When she came to the microphone to report her healing, we asked her if she was saved, and she said, "I am NOW!"

From ANDERSON, INDIANA . . . . . came an exciting letter: "The miracle you prayed for our family has arrived! Our son's recovery from drugs is really great!"

That was an exciting moment in their lives because they NEEDED A MIRACLE!

The miracle they needed won't be yours, because God deals with each one of us individually, and each of our miracles is special to us.

"My hernia was healed during your miracle service."

"I was healed of diabetes after attending your meeting."

"I was healed of cancer of the colon."

"God restored the sight in my right eye."

"I had been paralyzed from a stroke for four years and was brought to your meeting and was instantly healed. Praise God!"

"After eleven years of wanting a baby, you prayed for us and we now have a beautiful boy! Thank you, Jesus, for our miracle!"

"You prayed for healing of my eight-pound tumor, and it instantly disappeared! Hallelujah!"

"My gout was instantly healed!!"

These are all from letters in our office, and represent a BIG miracle to each one because IT WAS THE ONE THEY NEEDED!

Your miracle is a BIG one, because it's the one YOU NEED!

Let's agree right now and believe that THIS IS YOUR DAY FOR A MIRACLE! Lay your hands on ours, will you?

> Dear friend, we pray for you right now. We agree with you that whatever your need is, Jesus Christ will undertake for you at this very moment. We believe for your miracle just like those recorded in this book. As our hands touch, we ask God to release the miracle power of his Holy Spirit — NOW! Because we've asked in Jesus' name, we believe and thank God for your
>
> IMPOSSIBLE MIRACLE!

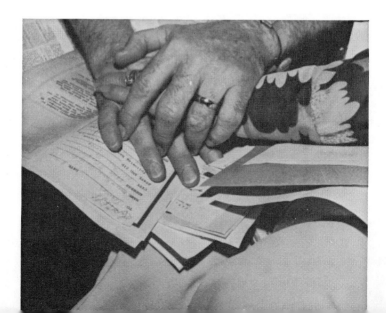